The Mirror Guide to

BUYING
A HOUSE

The Mirror
Money Series

The Mirror Guide to Managing Your Money

John Husband

Do you pay too much tax? Claim all your benefits? Understand what an APR is? *The Mirror Guide to Managing Your Money* is packed with financial advice on how to make the most of your cash, all in plain English. It's like having your own financial advisor in your pocket!

£5.99 ISBN: 0-13-915802-2

The Mirror Guide to Buying a House

Diane Boliver

Buying a home is one of the biggest financial decisions anyone can make - and one of the most stressful. Let *Mirror Money* expert Diane Boliver talk you through the maze. There's plenty of advice for first time buyers and lots of tips to help you land your dream home.

£5.99 ISBN: 0-13-915794-8

The Mirror Guide to Tax

Shirley Davenport

Tax self-assessment is a pain no matter what you do for a living or how much you earn. Let Shirley Davenport, *The Mirror's* tax expert, help you to make it easier on yourself. There's plenty of coverage on self-assessment for the self-employed, who face a particularly hard time when filling out their tax returns.

£5.99 ISBN: 0-13-915810-3

The Mirror Guide to Investment

Ken Clay

Got a small windfall from the sale of your home or a building society merger? Inside *The Mirror Guide to Investment* you'll find great advice on how to invest wisely and get the best returns on your cash.

£5.99 ISBN: 0-13-915828-6

The Mirror Guide to

BUYING A HOUSE

Diane Boliver

in association with

Prentice Hall Europe

London   New York   Toronto   Sydney   Tokyo
Singapore   Madrid   Mexico City   Munich   Paris

First published 1998 by
The Mirror with
Prentice Hall Europe
Campus 400, Maylands Avenue
Hemel Hempstead
Hertfordshire, HP2 7EZ
A division of Simon & Schuster International Group

Typeset in 10 pt New Baskerville
by Fakenham Photosetting Limited, Fakenham, Norfolk

Printed and bound in Great Britain by Biddles Limited, Surrey

British Library Cataloguing in Publication Data
A catalogue record for this book is available from the British Library

ISBN 0-13-915794-8

1 2 3 4 5 02 01 00 99 98

CONTENTS

6
Checking It Out 61

7
Signed, Sealed, Delivered 73

8
The Big Move 83

9
Protecting Against Disaster 95

10
Home Improvements 107

11
Selling Up 119

12
Cashing In on Your Home 127

Jargon Buster 135

Useful Contacts 141

Index 145

This book is dedicated to
Henry, Ollie and Will
———————————

INTRODUCTION

The aim of this book is to make light work of what can be one of the most traumatising of all of life's experiences. Buying a house ranks alongside death and divorce. But it needn't be stressful if you are well prepared for it.

The book assumes that you have never bought before. Although Chapter 11 deals with selling which will be useful to those considering a step up the property ladder or jumping off it!

The British are a nation of housemovers. In fact, homeownership in Britain is higher than anywhere else in Europe. Nearly two-thirds of the population either own or are buying their own house. And of those, two out of three are likely to live in four or more homes during their lifetime, while up to half will move four to seven times during their lifetime.

Half of us will move less than 10 miles from where we were born. But for the one-in-four settling between 10 and 100 miles away, the move will involve huge upheaval.

In good times you will call your home your castle. But in times of recession, as in the early 1990s – when the property market nosedived and millions of homes were worth less than the loans secured on them, it could become a noose around your neck. The secret of home buying, therefore, is to know exactly what you are getting into and not to overstretch yourself.

As well as minimising stress, there are numerous hints on keeping your expenses down. Useful addresses and telephone numbers of organisations can be found at the back of the book as well as a glossary of terms or jargon often used in the house-buying process.

I have not included any details on the buying process in Scotland which is very different to England and Wales.

Happy ownership!

1

HOW MUCH CAN I BORROW?

Buying a house is one of the biggest financial commitments you will make. So it's important to get your sums right from the start before you even begin looking for that dream home.

Unless you win the lottery, the pools or your Premium Bonds come up, most people will need to borrow some money to get on the property ladder. How much, will depend on numerous factors.

Your Income

Most lenders restrict their lending to two and a half or three times the income of one borrower. So if you earn £15,000 you would be able to borrow £37,500 to £45,000.

Some lenders, including the Halifax and Cheltenham & Gloucester (C&G), may lend over four times your income. In doing so they will take into account your future earning capacity, your credit history and your job. A bank or building society is likely to look more favourably on you if you're a long-standing customer.

If you are buying with a friend, partner or spouse and you are both earning, the income multiple is generally two and a half or three times your joint incomes. Or sometimes three times the higher income and one to one and a half times the lower income.

The income is your gross before tax income and not based on what you take home at the end of the week.

Lenders will want to see that your income is regular. It's not worth lying about it as the lender will take up references from your work. It is worth telling them about any overtime if it's regular and about a pay rise that may be in the pipeline.

Your Savings

Although 100 per cent loans do exist, most lenders will want you to have a stake in the property. They will expect you to find a deposit of at least 5 per cent. So on a £50,000 property you will be expected to find at least £2500.

The bigger the deposit the less interest you will pay and you will often qualify for a better mortgage deal.

Tot up what you have saved in the building society or bank.

But be wary of cashing in any savings policies, like endowments, early. It is unlikely you will get back the full value of the policy. You can always consider paying off some of the mortgage when it does mature, which will generally be a much better bet.

Don't commit every penny of your savings to a house. Remember there will be plenty of additional house-buying costs and you should always keep something by in case of an emergency not necessarily related to your house.

Your Debts

The lender will want to know about other regular outgoings you have. These could be a personal loan or car purchase plan repayments or credit card debts.

It's important to be straight about these and a good idea to clear them if you can. The interest on these debts will be much higher than you will pay for a home loan.

If you ask, your lender may agree to let you add some of your existing debts to your home loan. But remember you'll be paying interest on them for up to 25 years.

There's no point in lying about other financial commitments when you apply for a loan: Your lender will 'credit score' you and use a credit reference agency to check your past credit history.

Purchase-related Costs

Solicitor's Fees

(See Chapter 6.)

Stamp Duty

This will be one of your biggest bills if the property you're buying is over £60,000. It is the tax you pay on the purchase price of houses.

On properties over £60,000 it is 1 per cent, on homes over £250,000 it is 2 per cent and over £500,000 it is now 3 per cent. So, on a property worth £60,000 there's no stamp duty, but on a property worth £60,500 it will cost you £605.

If the property you're buying is just over £60,000 it could be worth doing a bit of hard bargaining to get the price down.

Land Registry Fee

This has to be paid on all property sales. There is a scale of charges depending on the purchase price. See page 5 for costs.

Local Authority Searches

There is a fee charged for information about planning in the area you are buying. It's important. You could discover a major through road is planned for the bottom of the garden. Expect to pay at least £60, more for London.

ENGLAND AND WALES

House prices	Cost of selling		Cost of buying	
£25,000	Solicitor	£309	Solicitor	£322
	Estate Agent (sole agency)	£778	Land Registry	£40
			Searches	£91
			Stamp Duty	nil
			Home Purchase Report	£265
	TOTAL	**£1087**	**TOTAL**	**£718**
£50,000	Solicitor	£327	Solicitor	£344
	Estate Agent (sole agency)	£1009	Land Registry	£70
			Searches	£91
			Stamp Duty	nil
			Home Purchase Report	£265
	TOTAL	**£1336**	**TOTAL**	**£770**
£60,000	Solicitor	£343	Solicitor	£358
	Estate Agent (sole agency)	£1172	Land Registry	£90
			Searches	£91
			Stamp Duty	nil
			Home Purchase Report	£325
	TOTAL	**£1515**	**TOTAL**	**£864**
£80,000	Solicitor	£374	Solicitor	£389
	Estate Agent (sole agency)	£1533	Land Registry	£130
			Searches	£91
			Stamp Duty	£800
			Home Purchase Report	£340
	TOTAL	**£1907**	**TOTAL**	**£1750**
£100,000	Solicitor	£411	Solicitor	£430
	Estate Agent (sole agency)	£1891	Land Registry	£190
			Searches	£91
			Stamp Duty	£1000
			Home Purchase Report	£340
	TOTAL	**£2302**	**TOTAL**	**£2051**
£150,000	Solicitor	£473	Solicitor	£499
	Estate Agent (sole agency)	£2751	Land Registry	£220
			Searches	£91
			Stamp Duty	£1500
			Home Purchase Report	£400
	TOTAL	**£3224**	**TOTAL**	**£2710**
£200,000	Solicitor	£549	Solicitor	£583
	Estate Agent (sole agency)	£3625	Land Registry	£260
			Searches	£91
			Stamp Duty	£2000
			Home Purchase Report	£455
	TOTAL	**£4174**	**TOTAL**	**£3389**

Source: The Woolwich

LAND REGISTRY FEE	
Purchase price	**Land registry fee**
Under £30,000	£40
£30,001 - £40,000	£60
£40,001 - £50,000	£80
£50,001 - £60,000	£100
£60,001 - £70,000	£120
£70,001 - £80,000	£140
£80,001 - £90,000	£170
£90,001 - £100,000	£200
£100,001 - £150,000	£230
£150,001 - £200,000	£260
£200,001 - £300,000	£300

Other Disbursements

Charged by your solicitor, these will include things like bank transfer fees and other searches. Allow up to £70 for the average house.

Mortgage Valuation Fee

Your lender will want to instruct a surveyor to value the property. The surveyor will only comment on the condition of the parts of the house that are visible and accessible. It will not be a full investigation. But it may suggest to the lender that a full investigation or work is carried out before it lends money.

The survey is done basically to assure the lender that the condition and value of the house is in keeping with the amount of money you want to borrow to pay for it.

If in the lender's view the house is worth less than the purchase price, the amount of loan offered to you may be reduced. The surveyor may suggest to the lender that they withhold some money, which will be paid only when the work on refurbishing the property has been carried out satisfactorily.

If substantial amounts are involved it could be worth getting a second opinion, or renegotiating the price with the seller.

What you pay will depend on the purchase price of the house (plus VAT). But allow around £125 for a £50,000 house and £165 for a £100,000 house.

Between a full structural and mortgage valuation there is a house-buyer's report which your lender may offer. Expect to pay around £330 for a £100,000 house.

Full Structural Survey

In addition to the lender's survey you may want to have a more thorough, full structural survey carried out on the property, especially if it's an old house, say, in an area prone to subsidence.

It will generally be cheaper if you ask the lender's valuer to do this for you while he is doing the valuation for the lender.

Alternatively call the Royal Institute of Chartered Surveyors for a member firm local to you.

Another option is to ask friends or your solicitor or estate agent to recommend one.

There's a danger you'll have to fork out for more than one survey while you are house hunting. Because one survey may make you decide the house is unsuitable. Equally, you may be gazumped or the seller may take the property off the market, which means you'll have to start house hunting all over again.

Expect to pay anything from £250 to £1000 plus VAT.

Mortgage Indemnity Guarantee

If you can't find a 25 per cent deposit, it is likely you will have to pay a Mortgage Indemnity Guarantee (MIG), although some lenders have axed this if you can produce at least a 10 per cent deposit.

Many borrowers have never heard of it. Yet it can cost thousands of pounds and is compulsory where applied.

MIG is a form of insurance for the lender in case you default on the loan and the subsequent sale of your property doesn't cover

TYPICAL MIG CALCULATION

MIGs usually start being charged at 75% of the loan to value. So if you borrow 80% of the property's value, for example, you will be charged a premium on 5.1% of the loan (the difference between 75% and 80%). So, if you are buying a house worth £60,000 and want to borrow 80% (£48,000), using the typical example below, you will be charged 5.1% on the difference between £45,000 (75%) and £48,000 (80%).

£3,000 ÷ 100 x 5.1 = £153.00

Loan to Value	%MIG
75%	0.00
80%	5.10
85%	7.15
90%	8.50
95%	8.50

your debt. You pay the premiums yet you get no cover at all. In fact the lender is not even obliged to show you a copy of the policy document.

At the height of the recession when thousands of homeowners' homes were repossessed, there was outrage that the insurance paid for by the borrowers failed to cover them against the loss.

Even more outrageous is the fact that even though you, the borrower, pay the premium, the insurance company can make a claim against you personally for reimbursement if it has to pay out under the policy.

So some lenders – like C&G, Lloyds, and Hinckley & Rugby Building Society – don't charge MIG any more. And it's worth approaching them if you have a very small deposit.

Typically you'll pay at least 5 per cent of the amount of extra loan over 75 per cent of the property value. Most lenders will allow you to add the cost of this to the home loan. But it's better if you can pay it up front as interest will be charged on the extra debt if it is added to the loan.

Basically, the more you borrow, the larger the MIG and the higher the percentage of the property's value borrowed, the steeper the charges get.

Mortgage Arrangement Fee

This is typical on most mortgages that are not variable rate loans. So if you choose a fixed, capped, cashback or discounted deal, expect to pay anything from £100 to £400.

You must be wary because if you accept one loan offer, and a better deal later comes along, it is unlikely that the fee will be refunded. So check the small print. If it says non-refundable mortgage fee, you'll lose out if you change your mind.

Move-related Costs

The list may seem endless. But you have to take on board the fact that they exist before you work out how much you will need to borrow.

Services

There may be re-connection fees to pay when you arrive, especially if the property has been empty for some time. And you may need to employ a plumber or electrician when you move in to connect the washing machine or check the wiring.

If you are moving away from friends and family expect higher phone bills. You may also have to pay for the installation of a new

TYPICAL HOME BUYER'S BILL

	£50,000 property	£100,000 property
Stamp duty	n/a	£1000
Solicitor's fees	£600	£900
Searches	£25-£150	£25-£150
Land Registry	£80	£80
Solicitor's disbursements	£35	£35
Lender's legal fees	£300	£300
MIG	£500	£1,400
Lender's valuation	£110	£160
Survey fee	£300	£300
Buildings insurance	£100	£200
Removal firm	£300	£300
TOTAL	£2,475	£4,825

phone line or to take over the existing one. There won't be a connection charge if a line is unbroken between owners.

Removals

If you don't have a friend with a van, prepare for the cost of using a professional firm. It's worth contacting a few in your area for quotes.

Then compare that with doing it yourself. Contact a local van hire firm and get quotes for insuring your goods in transit. If you

COSTS AND EXPENSES OF MOVING

Basic checklist of expenses	Estimated £	Actual £
Maximum possible price to pay for house		
Solicitor's/conveyancer's fee		
Advertisments		
Estate agent's fee		
Land Registry fee		
Stamp duty		
Fee for local searches		
Other searches and disbursements		
Mortgage		
• Lender's solicitor's fee		
• Own solicitor's fee		
• Lender's valuer's fee		
• Top-up loan: charges		
• Mortgage indemnity policy		
Structural survey		
• Surveyor's fee		
• Fees for specialist tests		
Insurance		
• Buildings insurance premiums		
• Removals insurance premium		
Bridging loan		
• Bank's fee		
• Interest		
House hunting expenses		
• Transport		
• Accommodation		
• Time off		
• Other		
Removal expenses		
• Firm		
• Hire		
• Other		
Services		
• Disconnection		
• Reconnection		
• Installation of new equipment		
• Carpet laying		
• Mail redirection		
Incidentals		
• Change of address		
• Boarding animals		
• Meals out		
• Rewarding helpers		
• Telephone calls		
• Tips		
• Other		
• Contingency fund (% of total)		

already have a home contents policy your possessions will be covered for a move. But do check first.

Add in new curtains, carpets and furniture, essential repairs, change of address cards and any unpaid leave you may be taking from work and the costs really start adding up.

On-going Costs

Life Insurance

The lender will want you to have some form of life policy to cover the loan in case you die before it's paid off.

If you choose an endowment mortgage your life is covered by the endowment. If you choose any other form of mortgage you will need to buy life cover. The costs will vary depending on your age, sex and lifestyle.

But simple term assurance is generally quite cheap. To give you an idea at the time of writing, the best deals for a 20-year-old non-smoking male in need of £50,000 life cover for 25 years was as little as £3.75 a month, while for a 40-year-old the best quote was £13.

Premiums for women tend to be a few pounds cheaper, because statistics show they live longer. For obvious reasons smokers or people with ill-health pay more.

Premiums are normally paid monthly by direct debit from your account.

Don't be tempted by a lender finding a policy for you. There's every chance you can get a better deal by shopping around. Remember even the likes of Virgin Direct and M&S now offer life cover, so don't limit yourself to traditional insurers.

Council Tax

You probably have in mind the sort of place and area you want to live in. But it could be worth checking (with the local authority) council tax bandings of the sort of house you're looking to buy.

The lower the band, the less you'll pay. The lowest – Band A – covers properties under £40,000. The highest – Band H – covers any property over £320,000.

Remember you have the right to appeal against your council tax banding if you think it's too high, within six months of moving house. You can also appeal if you feel your property has been devalued by a new eyesore – a waste disposal plant at the bottom of the garden, for example.

Appeals should be lodged with a valuation tribunal, which can be contacted via the valuation office, which is listed in the phone directory.

But to win you need good, solid evidence that the eyesore has devalued your property.

Council tax bands use 1991 house price valuations, but a fall in the value of your house since, because of the state of the housing market, is not grounds for an appeal to be shifted into a lower tax band.

Insurance

Buildings insurance is a legal requirement. Your mortgage lender will want to know that you are covered against your home subsiding or having to be rebuilt after an explosion, for example.

Homes built on Britain's clay belt – which generally runs south of a line from Bristol to the Wash – are prone to subsidence and are likely to be charged more.

Home contents cover is not a legal requirement. But it's not worth the risk of not buying it. It will protect you against theft, fire and flooding and a raft of other possible disasters.

Travel Costs

Your journey to and from work could increase dramatically and involve buying a season ticket. Make sure you factor the extra costs in. Some employers provide staff with interest-free loans to buy annual travel tickets. So it could be worth asking.

Maintenance

When you own your own home, there will be no landlord to pick up the bill when the roof leaks or the paint starts peeling off the walls. It's worth setting something aside for maintenance and redecoration each year.

Services

Water charges, electricity and gas bills may all be bigger than you have been used to paying. When you view a property ask the owners for recent bills to give you an idea of the running costs of the house.

The Deposit

By now you should know from your income the amount of money a lender might consider giving you and the amount of money you could put down as a deposit.

The bigger it is, generally the better the mortgage deal you will be offered.

But don't forget you will be expected to hand over a 10 per cent deposit when you exchange contracts. On more expensive properties an agent may be able to negotiate a smaller amount, but 10 per cent is the norm.

Why Buy?

You wouldn't be reading this book if you weren't seriously thinking about buying. But already you've probably realised that it isn't a move that should be taken lightly.

It's worth asking yourself why you are doing it. If it's purely for profit, forget it now. While you should hope that your property rises in value it should not be the prime purpose for buying.

Also think about your job status. Is it really worth going

Net monthly repayments per £1,000 borrowed			
INTEREST RATE%	20 year term (£)	25 year term (£)	30 year term (£)
4.00	5.92	5.11	4.59
4.25	6.04	5.24	4.72
4.50	6.16	5.36	4.85
4.75	6.28	5.49	4.98
5.00	6.41	5.62	5.12
5.25	6.53	5.75	5.26
5.50	6.66	5.88	5.39
5.75	6.79	6.02	5.53
6.00	6.92	6.15	5.67
6.25	7.05	6.29	5.82
6.50	7.18	6.43	5.96
6.75	7.31	6.57	6.11
7.00	7.44	6.71	6.25
7.25	7.58	6.85	6.40
7.50	7.71	6.99	6.55
7.75	7.85	7.14	6.70
8.00	7.99	7.28	6.85
8.25	8.13	7.43	7.01
8.50	8.27	7.57	7.16
8.75	8.41	7.73	7.32
9.00	8.55	7.47	7.16
9.25	8.70	8.03	7.63
9.50	8.84	8.18	7.79
9.75	8.99	8.33	7.95
10.00	9.13	8.48	8.11

Gross monthly repayments per £1,000 borrowed			
INTEREST RATE%	20 year term (£)	25 year term (£)	30 year term (£)
4.00	6.13	5.33	4.82
4.25	6.27	5.48	4.97
4.50	6.41	5.62	5.12
4.75	6.55	5.77	5.27
5.00	6.69	5.91	5.42
5.25	6.83	6.06	5.58
5.50	6.97	6.21	5.73
5.75	7.12	6.36	5.89
6.00	7.27	6.52	6.05
6.25	7.41	6.67	6.22
6.50	7.58	6.83	6.38
6.75	7.71	6.99	6.55
7.00	7.87	7.15	6.72
7.25	8.02	7.31	6.88
7.50	8.17	7.48	7.06
7.75	8.33	7.64	7.23
8.00	8.49	7.81	7.40
8.25	8.65	7.97	7.58
8.50	8.81	8.14	7.75
8.75	8.97	8.31	7.93
9.00	9.13	8.48	8.11
9.25	9.29	8.66	8.29
9.50	9.46	8.83	8.47
9.75	9.62	9.00	8.66
10.00	9.79	9.18	8.84

through all the hassle of buying, if you know your job is likely to take you to another part of the country within the year?

Likewise, will the children be changing schools soon and take you to another town? Moving regularly can be very costly. Chapter 8 covers the cost of moving in different areas of the country.

2

WHAT SORT OF MORTGAGE?

Now you know how much you will need to borrow you should set about finding a lender who will lend it on the most favourable terms.

This is important to organise before you start house-hunting seriously. Because your dreams could be shattered if you find a place and need to move quickly to secure the deal.

A mortgage is a loan secured on your home. Unlike personal loans, which are unsecured, if you default on a mortgage (fail to make repayments on time) you risk having your home repossessed. So it is a commitment you must take very seriously. Once you have taken on a mortgage, you can't sell the house without first repaying the loan.

The world of mortgages is often described as a maze or a minefield.

It's not surprising. If you walked into a branch of the Halifax ten years ago – or any other bank or building society, for that matter – it would offer you just one mortgage. Now each lender has up to twenty different mortgage products from which you can choose.

Choosing a Lender

With well in excess of two hundred to choose from it's important to shop around.

But that doesn't mean walking the length of your local high street studying the offers. Numerous high street lenders now offer mortgages by phone. Even supermarkets and insurers are getting in on the mortgage act.

If you already have savings or a loan with a particular building society or bank, start with them first. They may give preferential deals to existing customers.

Although mortgages were traditionally the domain of building societies there is now very little difference between the products and terms offered by them and high street banks. Insurance companies offering mortgages, like Prudential, Legal & General and Direct Line, will be geared to flogging their own insurance policies, be it an endowment or buildings and contents policy.

Centralised lenders also offer loans, but there is evidence to suggest that if times get tough and you can't keep up your repayments, they are quicker to act than building societies and banks when it comes to repossession proceedings.

At the time of writing Sainsbury's was the only retailer to offer mortgages. And to date it only offers one product.

Many banks and building societies now have direct marketing where they sell over the phone. Because they have lower overheads than their branch-based counterparts the deals can be extremely good.

What's important to realise is that lenders will only sell their own products. Even estate agents selling mortgages may be owned by an insurance firm or bank and only sell their products.

If you want to find out who is offering the best rates to suit your particular needs, you should employ the services of a mortgage broker. If you pay the broker a fee, you are more likely (though not guaranteed) to get impartial advice. If you don't, he could be flogging the mortgage of a lender who pays him the biggest fee for introducing the business.

Unlike insurance brokers, who have to be registered with the Insurance Brokers Registration Council, anyone can set up in business and call themselves a mortgage broker or mortgage consultant. Good ones will belong to a body with a code of conduct for their members, and which will look into any complaint you may have.

Alternatively you can do the leg work yourself. To help, a publication called *Money£acts* produces a comprehensive monthly guide to every investment and mortgage rate on the market. As well as a Best Buy table, it details every mortgage deal on the market. Copies are generally available in good public libraries. Alternatively, see 'Useful Contacts' at the back of the book for details.

The Mortgage Term

It is typical to take out a loan over 25 years and repay the debt in monthly instalments.

That may be the norm. But the market is changing. And many lenders now allow and even encourage you to repay the debt over a shorter or longer term, depending on your age.

With some you can even repay in weekly instalments or over a 10-month year. Some allow repayment holidays – ideal if you are likely to take a career break to have kids.

So, if you are interested in paying your loan off early, ask your lender how much the repayments would cost over 20 years or 15 years. If you can afford them you'll save thousands of pounds in interest in the process (see 'Paying Your Loan Off Early', see p. 25).

Tax Relief

If the property you buy is to be your main home, you will get tax relief on the first £30,000 of the loan.

The relief, MIRAS (Mortgage Interest Relief at Source) has been restricted over the past few years. So, rather than getting tax relief at your highest rate – 23 per cent for basic rate taxpayers, 40 per cent for higher rate taxpayers – it is now only available at 10 per cent.

This means a saving of £210 a year.

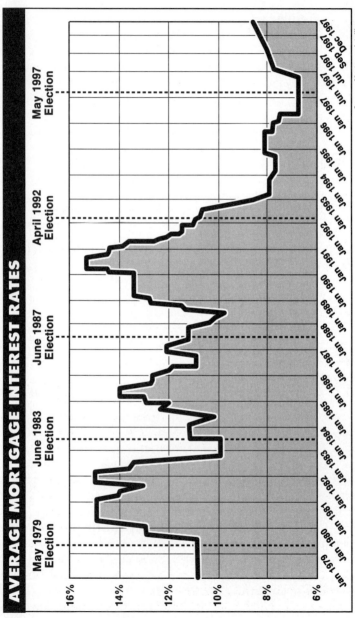

AVERAGE MORTGAGE INTEREST RATES

Source: Mortgage Intelligence

Interest Rates

When deciding which mortgage deal to take it's worth taking a view on interest rates.

If you have read and heard that interest rates are likely to go up in the near future, you should look to try and lock into today's rates. If they look likely to fall, it could be worth taking a mortgage whose interest rate will reflect the movement.

What is important is that you ask your lender what your repayments would be if interest rates rose by, say, 2, 3 or even 4 per cent. Could you still afford to pay them?

Historically, interest rates have always been high mid-way through a government's term in office, but then have fallen back at the time of a general election (see the illustration opposite).

Types of Mortgage

Fixed Rate Loans

Fixed rate loans are a phenomenon of the past 10 years or so.

They allow peace of mind in times of turbulent interest rate rises and falls. You literally lock in to a set rate of interest for a set term. So, if interest rates rise, you're a winner, If they fall, you could be paying over the odds. You know from the outset what your monthly repayments will be over that time.

However, they normally carry a booking or arrangement fee. And you should be wary of redemption penalties on the deal.

If a lender is offering a deal well below the market 'norm', there is likely to be a catch. And it will usually take the form of a redemption penalty. This means that if you decide you want to switch to another mortgage deal (redeem the mortgage early) within the fixed rate term you will have to pay a penalty. This can be as much as six months' interest.

Often lenders will also lock you into sticking with them long after the fixed term ends. You will also pay a penalty if you want to pay off a chunk of your loan early.

But fixed rates are well worth considering if you are stretching yourself to the limit and couldn't afford a rate rise.

Terms vary from six months to ten years. But be careful with short term deals. Make sure the deal lasts for six months from the date of completion and is not quoted with a date that runs out within six months of application. Sometimes it can take this long to complete on a house purchase by which time the offer will have run out.

Variable Rate Loans

Here your monthly repayments will fluctuate with interest rates generally. Borrowers who took out loans in the late 1980s will remember when interest rates almost doubled to 15 per cent within the space of just a few months.

The benefit of a variable rate loan is that if rates fall, you benefit. If rates go up, you pay more.

There are generally no fees to pay and you can redeem the loan at any time, which gives you the freedom to shop around all the time.

Most deals which allow you to pay chunks of your debt off early are nearly always variable rate loans.

Cashback Deals

Cashback deals are targeted at cash-strapped first-time buyers.

What they give you is much-needed extra cash at a time of great expense. It may allow you to buy a sofa, or kit out your house with curtains and carpets.

Cap and Collar Loans

These are great if you're not sure where interest rates are going. You know you will not pay more than the 'cap' and no less than the 'collar'. But what you pay will fluctuate with interest rate moves generally within those boundaries.

Discounted Loans

These offer a percentage off the loan for a set period of time.

So, if the going variable rate is 8 per cent and the discount is 2 per cent, you will pay 6 per cent.

If mortgage rates rise to 9 per cent, you will pay 7 per cent, and so on. But if they fall to 7 per cent, you pay 5.

First-time Buyer Deals

Keen to woo you, lenders often offer first-time buyers attractive deals.

Check the benefits.

For example, they may pay all your fees, give you an interest rate discount and some cashback.

Beware, though. Some deals for first-time buyers are not as attractive as deals available to all buyers.

100 per cent Loans

If you can't drum up a deposit, look to a 100 per cent loan. But think long and hard about the commitment.

Mortgage Conditions

With any mortgage deal always check the smallprint before signing up. Here you could discover a whole raft of clauses that might put you off. Important ones to look for are:

● **Redemption penalties** are imposed on numerous fixed-rate deals. They basically mean that if you redeem the loan, by moving to another lender or paying off more of the loan than you signed up to pay off within a set term, you will pay a penalty.

That can be anything from one month's interest to six months'.

● **Portability** is important. It means you will be able to take the mortgage deal with you if you move house.

● **Mandatory insurances** mean that by accepting the mortgage deal you also have to accept a lender's buildings and contents insurance or endowment or pension policy.

● **Mortgage Indemnity Premiums** (MIG) This is a fee charged to borrowers with loans of more than 75 per cent of the value of the property.

● **Application fees** can be charged to secure a fixed rate loan or other special deal. Find out whether they are refunded if you change your mind.

If You Are Turned Down

Don't give up hope if one lender turns you down. They will all have slightly different lending criteria.

If it's because you have a poor credit history or don't satisfy its income multiples, read Chapter 4.

Remortgaging

Once you have taken out a mortgage you don't have to stick with the same lender for the life of the loan. Many homeowners mistakenly believe they have to move house to move their mortgage. You don't. You can remortgage at any time.

But there will be costs involved.

These could include having a new survey done on your house, legal fees and possible fees on a new mortgage deal.

However, when lenders are desperate to capture a bigger slice of the market, they sometimes offer deals which pay all your costs to switch.

Paying Off Your Loan Early

You don't have to be saddled with a debt for 25 years once you've signed a mortgage agreement.

There is a growing breed of flexible mortgage lenders that actively encourage you to pay more than the minimum repayment each month. And you can save literally thousands of pounds by doing it.

Other lenders positively penalise against it with early redemption penalties of up to six months' interest.

So, if you are the type of borrower whose income fluctuates (perhaps you get a sizeable annual bonus each year or earn more at particular times of the year), it could be worth checking them out.

Some operate mortgage accounts in the same way as a bank account. You can overpay and even underpay or take a repayment holiday from time to time. The more you overpay while interest rates are low, the greater the savings.

Effect of Altering the Mortgage Term

A £50,000 mortgage over 25 years, assuming an interest rate of 7.99 per cent throughout, would cost £117,323.25 including the interest (£67,323.25) added. If you reduced the term to 15 years, the monthly payments would increase from £384 to around £486.49, but the total cost of the loan would decrease to £87,568.20 – a saving of £29,755.05.

So, for just over £100 a month extra, you can save nearly £30,000 and pay off your mortgage 10 years early.

Effect of Not Paying Monthly

If you pay £400 a month for 12 months you would pay £4800 a year, i.e. £400 × 12 = £4800.

If you halve that and pay fortnightly you would pay £200 × 26 = £5200 a year.

If you pay weekly you would pay £100 × 52 = £5200.

The difference between paying monthly and fortnightly or weekly is £400 over the year or an extra month's repayment.

Lenders offering flexible loans include Bank of Scotland Centrebank, Mortgages Direct, Clydesdale Bank, Legal & General, Mortgage Trust, Scottish Widows Bank, Royal Bank of Scotland and Yorkshire Bank.

The most radical lender by far is a flexible loan from Virgin Direct. It runs the 24-hour Virgin One telephone account which acts as your mortgage, bank, credit and savings account all wrapped into one with an 8.2 per cent (at the time of writing) interest rate.

To qualify you have to take out a mortgage of at least £50,000 and pay your salary into the account. Then you tot up all your debts, including mortgage, car loans and credit cards and Virgin lets you borrow 5 per cent on top of the total. Whatever you pay in goes towards clearing your debts, which is ideal for anyone wanting to pay their mortgage off early.

The account also offers everything you would expect of a traditional bank account, from cheque book and Visa card to standing orders and direct debit facilities.

Most mortgage lenders, including the Halifax, Nationwide and Bradford & Bingley, don't openly encourage you to pay more than your set monthly mortgage repayment unless you are in negative equity (when your property is worth less than your loan).

They do, however, allow it but you have to ask. And you will need to find out when they adjust interest payments. It's generally just once a year.

So, if you overpay every month throughout the year, your money will simply sit in the account doing you no good whatsoever. If that's the case it would be a much better idea to save the cash in a high interest savings account until just before the capital adjustment date and then transfer it.

The Negative Equity Trap

At the height of the property price slump of the early 1990s well over a million families lived in properties worth less than the loans on them. As a result, numerous lenders offered rescue packages to borrowers who wished to move. But not all qualified and many are still victims unable to trade out of their problems.

If you fall victim make sure you talk to your lender immediately.

Don't fall into arrears. They're unlikely to be sympathetic about your situation.

If you want to move, you may be able to take out a mortgage of up to 125 per cent of the value of the new home. But that's only likely if you have a clean repayment record.

Use some of your savings to reduce the loan, but don't touch your emergency funds.

You could consider converting an endowment mortgage to a repayment loan and selling on the policy to help you reduce your debts. But you will certainly get back less than the policy is worth and if it has not been running very long you may not even get back the money paid in to date.

So, if you can afford the extra expense you may be better off switching to a repayment loan AND keeping up the payments on the endowment policy.

If you are planning to rent, try to convert the negative equity into a personal loan.

If your lender isn't sympathetic to your plight, look at lenders that offer free-standing negative equity schemes to borrowers of other lenders. These include Barclays Bank (you need to have been a current account customer for two years), Cheltenham & Gloucester (minimum three years good repayment record required) and Bank of Scotland Centrebank.

3

HOW SHALL I REPAY THE DEBT?

So, you've chosen the sort of mortgage you want. Now you must consider how you want to repay the debt.

There are numerous options. But never be afraid to ask if you don't fully understand what is being said. Otherwise you could end up with the wrong deal.

Here we outline the main ones.

Repayment Loan

This is probably the best option for most people, especially if you like the idea of chipping away at the debt every month for the life of the loan.

Each month you will pay off interest and some of the capital. Although, in the early years most of what you pay each month goes to pay interest and only a small part goes towards paying off the capital. This swings in favour of capital as you near the end of the mortgage term.

Repayment loans are generally ideal for first-time buyers who want to build up some equity in their home, so that when they move on, they will have a bigger deposit to put down.

However, they may not be so good if you move very regularly, because you make very little capital repayment in the early years of the loan.

A way round this is to stick with the term of the original loan. When you move you simply pay off the loan when you sell your house with the money you get from selling it. If you are buying a new home, you then get a new mortgage deal for that.

Pros

● Easy to understand

● Loan is guaranteed to be repaid

Cons

● Need to start a new loan each time you move

● Separate life assurance is required

Interest-only Loans

With interest-only loans you don't pay off any of the capital. As the name implies, the monthly payments to your lender during the whole life of the loan comprise solely of interest.

You don't actually repay any of the outstanding debt until the end of the mortgage term (usually 25 years). To do that you invest separately in a savings policy. This could be anything from an endowment, personal equity plan to a pension. These are designed to build in value over the course of your loan so that they are worth enough to pay off your debt at the end of the loan term (see below).

The illustration on page 32 is designed to help you work out the monthly cost of an interest-only loan over 25 years. (You may want to compare it with the figures in Chapter 1 which covered payments on a repayment mortgage).

The first column shows the interest rate.

Column A shows how much you will have to pay per £1000

borrowed for mortgages up to £30,000 (the figures take into account MIRAS, or tax relief, at the current rate of 10 per cent).

Select the interest rate that applies to your loan and look across to the figure in Column A.

Then multiply this figure by the number of thousand pounds you wish to borrow.

Column B shows the gross amount you will have to pay each month.

Use this to calculate the interest on the portion of the mortgage over £30,000.

Example   If you want to borrow £55,000 at 7.25 per cent, look at column A and multiply 5.14 × 30 (= £154.20). Then using Column B multiply 6.04 × 25 (= £151). Add the two together to give you your monthly repayment (= £305.20).

Endowment

Endowment policies used to be the most popular investment plan used to pay off a mortgage. Figures from the Office of Fair Trading show how their popularity steadily grew from only 6.7 per cent of the market in 1970 to a huge 75 per cent by 1990. In the 1980s the returns from them more than covered the loan and gave investors a fabulous tax-free lump sum on top.

The building society tie-ups with life insurance companies of the 1980s were to blame for their surge in popularity. Life companies paid huge commissions on the sale of an endowment – typically around two-thirds of all the first five years' premiums. In some cases it was even more, with some salesmen earning £1500 per mortgage.

Recommending a repayment mortgage earns the broker nothing. But these policies are not without their faults. In fact, I consider them one of the worst investment products of all time.

Firstly, they have been massively oversold and often to the wrong sort of borrower. That's because salesmen can earn more commission selling an endowment than any other product. In fact, a salesman could take up to 80 per cent of what you invest in the first year.

Secondly, they only prove good value if you stick with them for

Monthly repayments per £1,000 borrowed		
INTEREST RATE%	With tax relief (A)	Without tax relief (B)
4.00	3.00	3.33
4.25	3.20	3.54
4.50	3.38	3.75
4.75	3.57	3.96
5.00	3.75	4.17
5.25	3.95	4.37
5.50	4.13	4.58
5.75	4.32	4.79
6.00	4.50	5.00
6.25	4.70	5.21
6.50	4.88	5.42
6.75	5.07	5.62
7.00	5.25	5.83
7.25	5.45	6.04
7.50	5.63	6.25
7.75	5.82	6.46
8.00	6.00	6.67
8.25	6.20	6.87
8.50	6.38	7.08
8.75	6.57	7.29
9.00	6.75	7.50
9.25	6.95	7.71
9.50	7.13	7.92
9.75	7.32	8.12
10.00	7.50	8.33

the whole 25 years. That, in this day and age, is a difficult task. Jobs for life no longer exist. People's circumstances change so much and endowments take no account of the fact that you may have to stop paying premiums for a few months.

They are also what is called 'front-end loaded'. This means that the charges on the policies are all paid in the early years. So, if you cash in an endowment within five to seven years of taking it out, you are hardly likely to get back what you've paid in.

No more than 20 per cent of endowment mortgages are held for their 25-year term. In fact 18 per cent – that's about £3 to £4 billion worth – are cashed in during the first year and most don't survive more than seven years.

The insurance industry has made a scandalous killing out of them.

Endowment policies have a savings and life insurance element.

Young people with no dependents don't need life insurance. So it's criminal if they are sold endowments. They are totally inflexible. They take no account of the fact that redundancy or a split with a partner could mean money is tight and premiums can't be kept up.

Often the value of an endowment in year 24 can double in its final year. So unless you keep it for the full term you miss out massively.

If you struggle to pay endowment premiums, rather than cashing in your endowment you could consider making the policy 'paid up'. This means it continues to attract annual bonuses on what you've paid in, so you still get something when it matures.

Alternatively, there is a thriving second hand market in endowment policies. In general, a second-hand trader will give you 15 per cent more for your policy than you'd get if you simply surrendered it back to the company that issued it.

Not all policies are saleable. And even saleable with-profits policies have to have run for at least five years or a fifth of their life and have a surrender value of at least £1000 to £2000.

(For a list of policy market makers contact the Association of Policy Market Makers, telephone (0171) 739 3949. *Traded Endowment Policies – All Your Questions Answered* is available free from Policy Portfolio, telephone (0181) 343 4567.)

Another little-known option if money is tight, is to borrow against your policy.

Around 80 firms are prepared to secure loans against the surrender value of a policy. And the interest charged is generally much lower than you'd pay on a personal loan. The minimum loan is £100 and the maximum is generally 90 to 95 per cent of the surrender value.

Often the interest doesn't have to be paid immediately and can be rolled up and deducted from the policy value when it becomes a claim on death, surrender or maturity. In most cases, loans can be paid off at any time without penalty.

If after all this you still think an endowment is the right thing for you make sure you shop around for a decent one! Don't just accept the one offered by your lender.

Remember, only the Bradford & Bingley and Yorkshire building societies offer independent financial advice on the high street. The rest will push the product of one company only. And they will always use statistics that flatter its performance.

Always question the amount of commission the salesman will earn from flogging the endowment to you. They are obliged to tell you.

Remember, they won't get a penny from you if you choose a repayment loan.

According to *Money Marketing* magazine, which annually reviews the performance of 25-year endowments, the difference between the best and worst performers can be as much as £30,000 when they mature. Ignorance about endowment mortgages is reckoned to cost homeowners £50 to £70 million a year.

There are a few different types.

● A **non-profit endowment** ensures your debt is repaid at the end of the term but gives you no more than that.

● A **with-profits** endowment also guarantees to pay enough to cover the capital borrowed, but in addition will share in the profits made by the company as a result of investing your premiums. Each year the policy attracts annual bonuses which can't be taken away. So even if investment returns fall you have locked in the gains made in previous years.

● A **low-cost endowment** is also a with-profits policy, but much cheaper. It only guarantees to pay off about half of the mortgage. The hope is that the rest of the loan will be covered by profits made by their investment fund.

   In the 1980s this seemed a pretty safe option. But during the recession of the early 1990s and times of lower investment returns, numerous borrowers with endowment mortgages were forced to increase their premiums for fear that the policy would not repay the debt at the end of the term.

● **Unit-linked endowments** are more risky. Here your money is invested in shares. There are no annual bonuses that enable you to lock in gains made in good times. The value of your investment simply reflects the fortunes of the stockmarket and the ability of the fund manager. So, if in the year your mortgage matures stockmarkets take a nosedive, you could lose out. Conversely you have the chance to make a considerable profit if times are good.

Pros

● Built-in life cover
● Potential for tax-free lump sum surplus after loan is repaid
● Possible early repayment of your loan

Cons

● Value of endowment may not be sufficient to pay off your mortgage
● May have to increase premiums to cover potential shortfall

Personal Equity Plan

Personal equity plans, or PEPs, as they are better known, are simply a tax shelter through which you can invest in shares. They have become an increasingly popular way to pay off a mortgage.

   The plan can be a direct investment where you pick the stocks or an investment in a unit or investment trust, which are funds which invest in a range of shares. They suit higher rate taxpayers.

Any investment in shares is risky. And there is no guarantee that there will be enough money to repay all your debt. But history suggests that it's not so risky if you invest over the long term. Any investment in shares should always be considered over the long term.

In fact, over every five-year period since the Second World War, shares have outperformed the returns from other forms of saving, such as building societies.

What is fantastic about PEPS is their flexibility. Another good thing about using them to pay off a home loan is that as soon as your PEP grows enough you can pay off your mortgage debt.

Under current rules you can invest up to £6000 each year (twice that for a couple) in a general PEP and another £3000 a year (twice that for a couple) in a single company PEP or the shares of just one company.

But the Government plans to scrap PEPs in April 1999 and replace them with tax-free Individual Savings Accounts with a yearly limit of £5000 instead of £7000 in the first year. PEP investors will be allowed to keep their PEPs and contribute to an ISA. That should be enough to cover most PEP mortgages.

Do seek advice from your mortgage provider first.

Most banks and building societies now offer PEPS. But, beware. None has ever made it into any Top 10 performance tables. As with endowments it's best by far to talk to an independent financial adviser specialising in them. They will be able to scour the market to find a PEP best suited to your needs and attitude to risk.

A number of these are listed under 'Useful Contacts'.

Pros

- Tax-free investment
- Possible surplus lump sum
- Possible early repayment

Cons

- Separate life cover may need to be arranged

● Tax-free benefits not guaranteed
● No guarantee the loan will be paid off

Pension

Like an endowment and PEP mortgage, in addition to the mortgage interest you pay regular premiums to a pension plan. When
you start drawing your pension, part of it can be taken as a lump
sum and used to pay off the mortgage, the rest providing you with
a regular income in your retirement.

The advantage is that as well as tax relief on the interest on the
mortgage loan, you also get tax relief (at your highest rate of tax)
on your pension contributions. So for every £100 you pay it
actually only costs a higher rate taxpayer £60 and a basic rate
taxpayer £77.

But there are pitfalls. With people surviving longer, you could
find you need all of your pension not to pay off your mortgage, but
to live on in your old age.

You may also be tying yourself to retiring at a set time in the
future. Few lenders will give pension mortgages to young people
who intend to retire 35 to 40 years in the future.

They are best suited to the self-employed or employees with
personal pensions. But, remember, the amount of earnings that
can be paid in pension contributions to qualify for tax relief is
limited.

Pros

● Tax-efficient investment

Cons

● Uses valuable retirement funds

What If I Move?

If you move before your endowment or pension plan has paid out,
the loan will have to be repaid from the proceeds of selling your

old home. You can then link the mortgage on a new home to the endowment or pension plan you have.

If the loan is bigger you may need to increase your premiums or take out another policy to cover the extra debt. Alternatively, you could take out an alternative policy like a PEP to run alongside your existing investment plans.

Questions You Must Ask Your Lender

● How flexible is the loan?

● Will there be any penalties if I want to increase or decrease my payments each month?

● What about life insurance, if I die during the term of the mortgage?

● Can I shop around for the best savings policy and insurance products for me?

● When and how will payments have to be made?

● What happens when the interest rate changes?

● What would I have to pay if interest rates rose by, say, 3 per cent?

Applying for a Loan

Once a lender has established your income and commitments, they may give you a mortgage certificate.

This states how much they would be prepared to lend, subject to the value of the property you want to buy. This constitutes an offer to lend, but it is usually only valid for about six weeks to three months.

It can be useful proof to convince a seller that you are a serious buyer and have a mortgage in the pipeline. Before a lender gives it to you he will have checked with your bank, your employer, landlord and any previous mortgage lender to confirm the details you have given and to check that you are creditworthy.

The Code of Mortgage Lending

A code of mortgage lending practice exists to protect anyone buying a home. It sets out minimum standards that lenders must operate in respect of how they advise customers and the way they operate accounts.

The Code – issued by the Council of Mortgage Lenders (CML) – also requires all members of that body, which represents 98 per cent of the industry, to belong to an independent complaints system, free of charge for users. As yet, however, there is no statutory regulation, similar to the rules governing the sale of life and pension products.

The Code sets out three different levels of service which might be provided by lenders. These are:

● Information only on the mortgage product chosen by the borrower

or

● Information on a range of the lender's products

or

● Advice and a product recommendation

You should be told at the outset what levels of service are available. If a lender is providing a recommendation, they must be able to explain why they are promoting one product over another.

And the advice, which may initially be verbal, must also be given in writing.

The problem with the Code is that it does not cover intermediaries like mortgage brokers, independent financial advisers, estate agents, housebuilders, solicitors and accountants.

And evidence suggests that around half of all borrowers get recommendations from intermediaries instead of talking directly to lenders.

Many intermediaries have adopted the code. For a list of those that do subscribe contact the Council of Mortgage Lenders at 3 Savile Row, London W1X 1AF. There is a recorded consumer information line on telephone (0171) 440 2255.

4

WHAT IF I'M A HIGH-RISK BORROWER?

Mortgage lenders are adapting to the changing employment market. So, if you are on a short-term contract, self-employed or do freelance work, don't panic.

You may still be able to get a home loan. Lenders are coming round to the fact that although thousands of people came unstuck during the recession, many have since had an unblemished credit history.

If you are turned down by one lender, don't panic. There are numerous new mortgage lenders which specialise in higher-risk borrowers. But you may need to employ the services of a broker to find one.

Brokers will have details of all lenders on computer and once they have established what proof of income you can provide, they can work out which lenders will consider your application and what the best deals are, depending on the type of mortgage you want and the size of deposit you have to put down.

They will also be able to act as a 'buffer' between you and the lender, helping to smooth over any problems that may come up during application. Expect to pay around 1 per cent of the mortgage advance in fees, although commissions made on any insurance, pension, endowment or other financial products arranged through them will usually be discounted against this, which often results in no direct fee.

Self-employed

Many of Britain's 3.25 million self-employed often have problems meeting the strict lending criteria of high street lenders.

Without the usual PAYE payslips or P60s, you will usually have to come up with three years of accounts, which effectively rules out anyone who hasn't been self-employed for at least three years. Even if you have three years' accounts your accountant may have played down your profits in order to minimise your tax liability – in full accordance with the GAAP (Generally Accepted Accounting Practice), of course!

This means that your business may not look as healthy on paper as it truly is, and the amount a lender will offer you (usually three times your annual income) will be reduced as a result.

You may find that some lenders won't choose to acknowledge that a self-employed borrower may well be able to afford higher repayments than accounts strictly show.

This rigid attitude has tended to grow over the years. In the late 1980s most lenders offered 'self-certificated' home loans. Potential borrowers were asked to produce either three years' accounts, tax assessments or an accountant's letter as proof of income, but each case was assessed on its merits.

Most lenders no longer offer these. Instead, some will want to see proof that your business turnover (sales) shows an increase each year and they may want to see business plans for future years. Others may take typical annual income as an average from over the last three years and will not increase the amount they will lend from three times that figure.

There are, however, a handful of lenders who are starting to take a more flexible view and who are well aware that jobs for life are a thing of the past.

Some will treat applicants with only two years' accounts as 'full status' and will therefore offer them all their usual mortgage products and advance up to 95 per cent of a property's value. They effectively allow you to state your own income, provided it is backed up by either an accountant's reference or bank statements.

However, in these circumstances lending will probably be

restricted to 75–80 per cent of a property's value, so a higher level of deposit will be required than for an ordinary loan.

Lenders will probably also want to see a reference from a previous lender or a letting agency and a record of the fact that you can keep up regular payments. They will also expect clear credit searches and most will require you to have been in business for at least two years.

Exceptions include the Kensington Mortgage Company which will offer loans of up to 80 per cent after just one year's trading, providing you can come up with an accountant's reference.

UCB will advance up to 75 per cent of loan to value (LTV) after one year's trading. Contract-based workers can get a loan from Kensington as long as they have at least one month left on their contract.

You may stand the best chance of success if you ask the bank that has a record of your payments for a home loan.

Self-certification – Details of Income Required But not Proof

Worth approaching: Capital Home Loans, First National Building Society, Household Mortgage Corporation (HMC), Irish Permanent, Kensington Mortgage Company, Mortgage Express, Mortgage Trust, National Counties Building Society, Sun Banking Corporation, The Mortgage Business, UCB Home Loans Corporation (source: *Money£acts*, November 1997).

Non-status Loans – No Details of Income Required

Worth approaching: Bank of Scotland, Bank of Scotland Centrebank, Bank of Scotland Mortgages Direct, Mortgage Express (source: *Money£acts*, November 1997).

Bad Debts

Business failure and marriage breakdown are the two major causes of ruined credit. But don't despair. A growing number of lenders are still willing to take you on.

One such is Paragon Mortgages which offers a Freshstart Mortgage. It will make exhaustive enquiries into your financial position to gain a clear view of where you stand now and more importantly in the future. It allows you to borrow up to 80 per cent of the value of the property and no limit is placed on the number of previous adverse credit incidents.

But you must be wary of who you talk to.

In February 1997, the Office of Fair Trading expressed concern about the poor lending practices of some firms who encouraged borrowers with poor credit ratings by offering second mortgages. In July 1997 it went as far as to warn lenders that they risked losing their credit licences if they didn't clean up their acts.

Some charged oppressive dual interest rate policies – one rate if you kept up with payments, another often twice as high if you missed just one payment – plus excessive fees and penalties for early repayment.

Kensington Mortgage Company will lend up to 90 per cent of a property's value to borrowers with one county court judgement (up to £1000) against them.

The following lenders are also understood to consider **minor** county court judgements (preferably cleared) and small arrears cases. All, however, say that each case is treated individually and at the manager's discretion. So if one turns you down, try another.

Abbey National, Barclays Bank, Birmingham Midshires Building Society, Bradford & Bingley Building Society, Bristol & West, Cheshire Building Society, Darlington Building Society, Hanley Economic Building Society, HMC, Lambeth Building Society, Manchester Building Society, National Counties Building Society, Nationwide Building Society, Newcastle Building Society, Paragon Mortgages, Saffron Walden Building Society, Stroud & Swindon Building Society, The Mortgage Business, Wesleyan Home Loans, Yorkshire Building Society. (source: *Money£acts*, November 1997).

Check Your Credit File

If you have a history of bad debts, it could be worth checking out your credit history before you talk to a lender. Each year hundreds of thousands of Britons are refused credit ... often because information held on them is incorrect.

When you apply for a mortgage the lender wants to find out first whether you are likely to repay the debt. Its decision is based on a process of credit-scoring. This takes into account your age, job and how long you have lived at your present address.

The lender is also likely to use a credit reference agency which lists details of previous loans, any county court judgements against you over the past six years, and whether you have been bankrupt or had your home repossessed.

The Office of Fair Trading reckons that incorrect details are held on the files of up to 200,000 people. And, bizarrely, it is up to YOU to make sure it's right.

There are many ways that people can be wrongly blacklisted. If you have had a county court judgment against you, but have since cleared the debt, a credit reference agency search will show the judgment but is unlikely to show the debt has been cleared.

It is up to you to prove repayment by sending a 'certificate of satisfaction' from the county court.

Some people have been blacklisted because they have been linked to people with a similar name. Others find their address has been blacklisted because of a previous occupant. You can write to the agency to disassociate yourself. But you will need to provide proof.

Consumers refused credit have the right to be given an indication of the reason why. The lender must tell you which credit reference agency it used. You have a right to see their information. If it seems okay, go back to the lender and find out whether its refusal was due to its credit-scoring method or its previous experience of you as a customer.

You have the right to appeal. It is often worth questioning a refusal.

If a credit reference agency has inaccurate information on

you, write a notice of correction, giving reasons why it is incorrect. Use no more than 200 words. If you hear nothing within 28 days, complain to the Director General of Fair Trading, Field House, 15–25 Bream's Buildings, London EC4A 1PR.

If you have been turned down for a loan because of incorrect information held on you, it is the agency's responsibility to send your amended file to the lender.

Credit Reference Agencies

Consumer watchdogs at *Which?* reckon credit reference agencies (CRAs) could be breaking the law.

In a survey of over 100 people it found eight people's files held information about family members illegally.

Serious mistakes were found on another nine, while one woman's file even said she owed £1637, even though the debt had been cleared years before.

CRAs include in our files details of all the people with whom we are financially linked. So, if you have a joint mortgage with a partner, his or her details will be on your file.

The law also allows for financial information about members of your family who have lived with you in the past to be included. Not only can this harm your chances of getting a loan if they paid their bills late, but also should your details be on their files they can find out information about your financial commitments.

The Consumers' Association reckon that CRAs should only be allowed to include financial details about people with whom you shared your last address, not any previous address, which is how CRAs interpret the law. It has asked the Data Protection Registrar to investigate.

How to Check Your Credit File

To check your credit rating, write to the agencies Equifax Europe,

Dept 1E, PO Box 3001, Glasgow G81 2DT and Experian, Consumer Help Service, PO Box 40, Notts NG7 2SS.

Send a £1 fee and details of your past six years' addresses.

The Office of Fair Trading has produced a booklet called *No
Credit?* For a free copy, telephone (0181) 398 3405.

Problems with Mortgage Payments

Losing your job or a marriage breakdown are the big causes of
arrears – and repossession.

So what do you do if you face running into mortgage arrears?

- Don't fool yourself the problem will go away. Contact your
  lender before you miss a payment – not when you have fallen
  six months behind.

- Negotiate to suspend, defer or cut your payments by
  extending the pay-off period. Some lenders will allow you to
  extend the term of a mortgage to up to 40 years, which will
  drastically cut your monthly payments to help clear the debt.

- Don't agree to settling the arrears in 18 months or even two
  years' time.

- If you get a court summons – don't ignore it.

- Don't panic and hand in your keys or abandon your home –
  you still owe money.

- Don't be tempted by advertisements offering second loans to
  pay off the first.

- If you are getting nowhere with your mortgage lender, talk to
  your local money advice centre or Citizens' Advice Bureau.

5

HOME-HUNTING

So you know how much you have to spend. Now it's time to get down to the serious business of finding a dream home that matches your purse.

What You Want

This is the time for some serious soul-searching. Think about the things that are most important to you, your partner and your family.

It could be proximity to work, good schools, shops. The number of bedrooms and the size of the garden and whether it is south-facing. You may have a smart car and need a garage. You may want a new house or an old wreck to do up.

Draw up a 'must have' list and prioritise it.

Next draw up a 'would like' list. This could help in the decision process when it comes to tossing up between one property and another.

Where to Find It

Love them or loathe them, most of us will use an estate agent to find a house.

It's worth befriending them and letting them know exactly what you have in mind, how quickly you could move and how much you have to spend. The keener you appear, the more likely they are to see you as a serious buyer.

If you are buying locally, it will be easy to visit local agents in your area and sign up on their books. Don't restrict yourself to looking in the window of one agent. Shop around and get on as many mailing lists as possible. There won't be any fees. Estate agents make their money from sellers and act on their behalf.

If you are moving areas, you can find the names and addresses of agents in that area by looking through a local Yellow Pages or the local newspaper's property section. Again, get on to their mailing lists. The problem of not being on the doorstep means that by the time you get details of a property, someone locally who could view immediately could have beaten you to it.

The National Association of Estate Agents runs a National Homelink Service which puts you in touch with other Homelink members in the area you wish to move to.

A good estate agent ought to be helpful in preventing you from making a wasted journey to view a property that he realises you won't like. He should also be able to set up a number of viewings during one visit.

It's well worth your while spending some time in an area to get a feel for how busy certain streets are at different times of the day and night. If you just view at weekends you could miss out on the fact that a road is used as a busy cut-through by commuters during weekdays.

Don't rely solely on agents. Many people advertise their homes privately in the classified sections of newspapers. Find out which days the property sections are published. *Loot*, the freesheet, and *Exchange & Mart* also have property sections.

Another option is to advertise yourself as a buyer in the 'Wanted' column.

Alternatively you may want to employ the services of a property-finding firm. The Association of Relocation Agents should be able to put you in touch with a few.

Relocation agents should be able to view a property on your behalf and sift through the unsuitable ones. They may also be able to put you in touch with solicitors, surveyors and even make removal arrangements for you.

But you'll have to pay for it. Registration fees can be anything from £200 to £500 and then they may take between 1 and 1.5 per cent of the purchase price when contracts are exchanged.

Beware Agent-speak!

The Property Misdescriptions Act 1991 was introduced in 1993 to clamp down on misleading flowery language used by estate agents. Now they must describe a property accurately, without hyperbole.

Here are a few euphemisms they can no longer get away with.

Bijou pied à terre	Tiny. You won't be able to swing a cat
Easy to manage	Tiny. You won't be able to swing a cat
Full double glazing	On a very busy road
Very spacious	Cavernous, cold and draughty
Secluded	The shops are miles away
Reasonably priced	Overpriced
Stone's throw	A two-mile hike
Mature garden	Overgrown wilderness
In need of modernisation	A wreck

Checking It Out

So you've found a place you want to view. Ask the agent for an appointment.

If you get to the house and you decide you don't like the look of it, say so. There is no point wasting an agent's time.

Always take a notebook, the agent's particulars and a measuring rule so you can check dimensions.

Try not to be influenced by décor. Concentrate on getting a general impression of the scale and condition.

Will there be room for the children to play if you want to start a family? Will your furniture fit into each of the rooms? Where will you park your pushchair? If there are steps to the front door, will you be able to get a pushchair up them?

Try and imagine yourself living there. Don't let the estate agent rush you. But if you do have a favourable first impression ask the agent if you can go back and view it again, perhaps at a different time of day. Take a friend who will give you an honest view and different perspective.

No single house is likely to satisfy all your needs, so it's important to refer to your list of 'must have' and 'would like'.

Also think about how long you plan to stay in the house. And the chances of your being able to sell quickly if you plan to move again within a year or so.

Things to Consider

1. Is the location right?
2. Are there enough bedrooms?
3. Is the layout suitable?
4. What about heating, lighting and services?
5. What condition is the property in – inside *and* out?
6. What about the garden, garage, drive or roadway? Will you be able to park easily?
7. When will the house be available?
8. What essential repairs are needed and what's the likely cost?
9. What is included in the price?
10. What do the neighbours and their homes look like? This could affect your ability to sell the property on.

Questions You Must Ask

Hard as it may be, always try to think the worst about the property, its disadvantages as much as its assets.

● Is the property freehold or leasehold? If it's leasehold, what is the ground rent and how often is it reviewed? What about maintenance charges or repairs or redecoration?

● Are there any restrictive covenants on the use of the house?

- Do other people have a right of way through your garden? If there are any shared facilities – drives, roofs, hedges, fences, etc. – who is responsible for them?

- If there is land at the back, ask whether development on it is likely. If the house next door is empty ask why.

- Do commuters park in your street during the week?

- What about mess or noise from local shops?

- Have the owners been burgled? Is it an area of high crime?

- Would you feel safe walking home from the bus or train at night?

- What about heating and lighting? Ask to see fuel bills. Is the loft insulated, the walls damp-proofed and the wood free of dry rot?

- Ask to see guarantees and details of any structural work carried out. If a lot of work has been carried out, was proper planning permission applied for and granted?

- How old is the boiler, does it need a new roof, has it been rewired?

- Is there a TV aerial, is the house linked up to cable?

- Ask to see fuel bills.

- What council tax band is it in?

Things to Look For

- Damp patches on walls and ceilings.

- Cracks. Are they just plaster cracks or could they be a sign of movement? Has the house been underpinned?

- Do the doors fit properly?

- Are the walls bulging?

- Are the windows rotting and do they fit properly?

- Are the rugs and carpets hiding a multitude of sins?

- Look in the loft. Is the roof sagging? If it's a flat roof, when was it laid?

● If the house is newly painted, what are the owners trying to cover up?

● Are there any trees too close to the property that could cause subsidence?

Tips on Buying

1. Visit as many agents as possible. Most will not keep you on their mailing lists for longer than two to four weeks.

2. Find out about the seller. Ask the agent why they are moving. If it's for work purposes, it could be they need to move quickly and will accept an offer below the asking price if *you* can move quickly.

3. Choose and appoint a solicitor before you find a property. This shows an agent you are serious.

4. View as many properties as possible to get an accurate idea of prices. Most buyers end up buying something totally different from their original ideal.

5. Ask if the property has been under offer before. And if so why did the buyers pull out? How long has it been on the market? Has the price dropped? What is happening to house prices in the area generally?

6. Always view the house at different times of the day. A quiet country lane on a Sunday could become a racetrack in the week.

7. Beware of agents' estimates of building costs for renovation. Take your own builder along.

8. If you are buying a new house, and some of the houses near it and like it are occupied, knock on their door and find out whether they are happy with their buy. Ask whether the builder is good at putting right minor faults, etc.

9. Remember the old adage: location, location, location.
   Spend time in the area. Talk to the locals, visit the local

pub. Be wary of owners who play music while you view – they could be trying to hide the sound of nearby trains.

Check ordnance survey maps for footpaths, rubbish dumps. Is the fifteen-minute run to school more like thirty? Go to your local planning office. A proposed development a mile away won't show up on the local search that forms part of your solicitor's normal due diligence, nor will a road-widening scheme or by-pass.

10. Always make the offer through the agent, never directly to the seller. Owners tend to get emotional about their places. Never appear too desperate even if you are!

11. In normal circumstances try an initial offer of 80–90 per cent of the asking price. Then be prepared to increase it in small steps. And let the owners stew for a few days before increasing your offer. However, if you are aware that the property is in demand this tactic may not work.

12. Always use a surveyor used to dealing with the type of house you are buying. If he gives a low valuation, ask for a reduction in price to cover the cost of work.

    Get free quotes from local builders – word-of-mouth recommendations of builders are best.

13. Never let on to the agent that you might pay more money. Always make them believe that each offer you make is your final one.

14. Always ask for extras like carpets, curtains, fridge, cooker, greenhouse, etc., to be included in the price.

15. Never buy from friends.

Buying at Auction

For those who lose their homes it's a nightmare. But repossessions are proving a boon to people looking for a bargain. Snatched-back properties can be snapped up at auction at a fraction of their original price.

The advantage of buying at auction is that it's quick – the

property is legally yours from the moment the hammer falls. This means you can't be gazumped. And because the property is usually empty, you can start improvement work or even move in immediately.

But there are dangers. The cheapest properties will probably have been vandalised. They may even have had the kitchens and bathrooms ripped out. If you see a property you like, you might pay for a solicitor, a survey and spend time arranging a mortgage and then be outbid. You might get carried away and bid more than you can afford. And if you want to pull out of the deal, you'll lose your deposit and can be sued for the balance.

Here are some tips to help you buy for a knock-down price at auction.

- Visit a number of auctions to familiarise yourself with the proceedings.
- Arrange your finance well in advance.
- Be prepared to move quickly.
- Do lots of homework. Have a survey done and ask a solicitor to look into any potential legal problems.
- Ask your lender for a banker's draft. If successful, you'll have to pay 10 per cent immediately and then the balance in 28 days.
- Before auction day, double-check the property is still available.
- If you are nervous of bidding, ask your solicitor to do it for you.
- In general, estate agents say properties go for 10 to 15 per cent more than the guide price.

The Royal Institute of Chartered Surveyors publishes a free guide to buying and selling at auction. See 'Useful Contacts' for details. Auctioneers often have free leaflets for the novice, too.

Right to Buy

If you want to buy your council flat or house and have lived there for more than two years, you have the right to buy it at a substantial discount – up to 70 per cent off its market value.

The discount is worked out by totting up the number of years you've been a council tenant (maximum 30) although you don't have to have lived in the same place during that time.

The Department of the Environment publishes a useful leaflet, *Your Right to Buy Your Home.*

Ownership is the same as for any other house. But you must live in it for at least three years or lose some of the discounted price.

There may also be certain restrictions on the sale if the house has been modified for use by the elderly, for example.

To trigger your interest in buying, ask your local authority for form RTB1.

Housing Associations

Even if you can't afford to buy your first home in one fell swoop, you may still be able to get a foothold on the property ladder.

Housing associations are independent organisations, often run as charities, that offer schemes enabling local authority tenants to buy part of their home, with the housing association taking on the rest of the mortgage. In some cases you don't even have to be a local authority tenant to benefit. The initial share you can buy is usually between 25 and 75 per cent of the property's value and you can increase this amount until you own the house outright.

There are two main housing association schemes available: the Shared Ownership Scheme and the Do-It-Yourself Shared Ownership.

With the Shared Ownership Scheme, the association builds a block of flats or houses and then sells them. The buyers take out a mortgage on a percentage of the property (more than 25 per cent, less than 75 per cent) and then pay rent on the remainder of the home with the option to increase the amount they own.

With the DIY scheme you must be a local authority or housing association tenant but can choose to buy any property on the market, as long as it meets certain criteria. The housing association then buys the property and you take out a mortgage on part of it and pay rent on the rest.

Contact your local authority for details of housing associations in your area that may run such schemes.

Home Exchange

If you want to cut out estate agents, consider house exchange. Chains of swappers are less likely to break down and you could save up to £1000 in fees.

Housebuilders such as Barratt, Laing, Prowting and Wimpey are also involved in exchanges.

Barratt sells one in three of its new homes by taking the customer's previous home in part-exchange.

But few builders will pay the full market value of your home. Most typically pay between 5 and 8 per cent less than an independent valuation.

And they will expect you to pay around 25 per cent more than the value of your old property for a new one.

Making an Offer

Once you decide you want to buy, tell the agent you want to make an offer. He will then relay this to the seller.

You are not committed to anything. Make clear the offer is subject to contract and your having surveys done.

If there is any objection to this, don't proceed.

When making an offer, remember the seller will be asking the most they dare. And most will be prepared to come down slightly, unless there is unusually high demand.

Most first offers should be about 20 per cent below the asking price. But if you are really keen you may be prepared to pay over the odds to get it.

Your bargaining power will be better if:

● You have a mortgage certificate guaranteeing an offer of a loan
● A buyer has been found for your house
● You are a cash buyer and have already sold your place

Once your offer is made, an estate agent will ask for the name and address of your solicitor.

You may also be asked for a small deposit of a few hundred pounds, to show your intent. But you don't have to provide it. And if the deal falls through it will be returned.

6

CHECKING IT OUT

So you've made an offer. Don't lose your cool in the euphoria. There's still plenty that could go wrong.

Contract Races

If someone else is interested in the same property you should be kept abreast of their offer. The seller may want to accept the higher price, or may accept a lower offer from the buyer able to move the fastest.

Whatever the case keep your solicitor and mortgage lender informed of what is going on.

If both buyers are offering the same money, it is not uncommon for two sets of contracts to be sent out to the would-be buyers, and the first buyer to send a deposit and sign the contract gets the house.

Even after you have won in a race like this there is nothing legally binding on the seller to sell to you.

So, only take part if you think you have a really good chance of winning.

Employing a Solicitor

If you haven't one already you need to employ a solicitor or licensed conveyancer. Conveyancing is the legal word for the administrative process of transferring ownership of a property.

They will check out whether the seller is a bankrupt, whether there are likely to be any sitting tenants, disputes over boundaries, etc.

Always shop around for a conveyancer. Charges vary enormously. Solicitors and licensed conveyancers are free to charge what they choose. The Law Society recommends only that fees should be 'fair and reasonable' based on the value of the house, how complicated the transaction is, how much time is spent, the skill involved, the number and importance of documents involved, whether the land is registered or unregistered etc.

But a recent nationwide survey of 150 solicitors/conveyancers by Cumbria Trading Standards Department found a near £400 difference in quotes to buy a £75,000 house in Kendal, Cumbria.

Says Trading Standards Officer Phil Ashcroft, 'Close on a million homes were sold in England and Wales last year, which was worth £727 million to the legal profession.

'Many of the quotes we found were given exclusive of VAT, which can be very confusing.

'And we even found different offices of the same practice quoting different costs.

'Only 6 of the 18 legal practices with more than one office gave identical quotes irrespective of which office was contacted.'

So the message is to shop around, even within the same firm.

Word-of-mouth recommendations of a good solicitor could also be worth a lot.

And always make sure there won't be any extras. As a rough guide allow for up to 1 per cent of the price plus VAT or a flat fee.

The National Solicitors' Network, which has 250 member firms nationwide, offers a fixed-fee conveyancing service costing £295 for buyers and the same for sellers.

DIY Conveyancing

If you are determined to cut out as many costs in the house-buying process as possible you could consider doing your own legal legwork.

But it's not advisable for the majority of buyers. Don't consider it if you are not buying freehold, the property isn't a house, is part of a property, you buy the property at auction, or the seller is not employing a professional and doing the same as you.

And remember that if you are getting a mortgage, the saving may not be great, because you will still have to pay the lender's solicitor's charge. When you employ a solicitor they will normally do yours and the lender's work at the same time and charge an all-in fee. If you do it yourself, your bill for the lender's legal work will cost more.

You will need to be very organised and put everything in writing. And you'll need a whole host of legal stationery.

You must definitely not contemplate a DIY job if the property is:

● not freehold

● not registered

● not in England and Wales

● not a house

● part of a property

● sold at auction

● not wholly occupied by the seller

● new and being bought from a developer

● being sold by a divorcing or separating couple

● being sold by someone doing their own legal work too

The bible for DIY enthusiasts is *Bradshaw's Guide To House Buying, Selling And Conveyancing For All.* The book should be available in good bookshops.

Alternatively Castle Stationery, which has been selling DIY homeselling kits for 15 years, also has DIY conveyancing kits, costing £4 for sellers and £7 for buyers. It also stocks Joseph Bradshaw's book. Contact: Castle Stationery, Castle Books, 10 Blackdown, Royal Leamington Spa CV32 6RA. The book costs about £10.

Not surprisingly, solicitors don't think the practice should be encouraged and point to the fact that you could make a very expensive mistake. Having said that, if you are buying a house with woodland at the bottom of the garden, the fact that a developer has planning permission to build an estate there will not show up in the search, nor would any planning proposals at committee stage.

So even if you employ a solicitor to do searches it's well worth asking your own questions and digging deeper. Go to the planning office and ask about surrounding properties and plans in the pipeline.

Joint Ownership

If you are buying a house with someone else you should talk to your solicitor as to which sort of joint ownership is most appropriate for you.

Joint Tenancy

Under this arrangement, neither owner can sell without the other's agreement. If one dies, the survivor automatically inherits the other's share. This is often the prepared arrangement for married couples or for couples living together as man and wife.

Tenancy in Common

Here each joint owner is able to dispose of his/her share as he or she wishes. It is the preferred route of friends buying together who want to retain their independence. Joint tenants always hold the property in equal shares, but tenants in common can have unequal shares which reflect their contribution to the price of the property.

It is extremely easy to switch a tenancy in common arrangement into a joint tenancy arrangement, but the other way round is more complicated and would always involve the services of a lawyer.

Buying Freehold

If you buy a freehold property you are buying a piece of land and everything below it to the centre of the earth!

However it doesn't necessarily mean you can do what you will with the property. There may be restrictive covenants, so that you can't run a business from there, for example. Or there may be a right of way, such as a footpath for public use at the bottom of your garden which you are obliged to keep clear.

These should come up on the searches the solicitor carries out. Whatever you do, don't ignore them.

Buying Leasehold

If you are buying leasehold you are buying the property but not the land it is built on.

With a leasehold property it's important to check out who the freeholder is and details of the leasehold agreement. To the freeholder you will have to pay annual ground rent and possibly a sum of money for regular maintenance of the property.

Find out the full costs and when they next become payable.

In addition you must be careful not to double up on insurance. The landlord should be responsible for buildings insurance but may charge you a percentage of the bill. Find out who the insurer is and ask to see the policy details. If the insurer hasn't changed for a few years you could suggest they shop around for a more competitive quote.

If you buy a leasehold in a house – not a flat – and the lease is running out, you have the right to acquire the freehold or a lease for a further 50 years. The right is only available to tenants who have lived in the property for the preceding three years or three of the past 10 years.

To apply you need to serve notice on the landlord before the lease expires. The landlord can refuse to give a new lease or to sell the freehold, but only on very narrow grounds, e.g. he needs the house more than you.

Mortgage Valuation

Your lender will want to instruct a surveyor to value the property. But before you let them know that you've found a property you must decide whether you want to get the same surveyor to carry out a more extensive home buyer's report.

Alternatively you may want the same surveyor to carry out a full structural survey. You ought to be able to negotiate a discount on such a deal, because all the work can be carried out in one trip.

For a simple mortgage valuation survey, the surveyor will only comment on the condition of the parts of the house that are visible and accessible. It will not be a full investigation. But it may suggest to the lender that a full investigation or work is carried out before it lends money.

The survey is basically done to assure the lender that the condition and value of the house is in keeping with the amount of money you want to borrow to pay for it. If, in the lender's view, the house is worth less than the purchase price, the amount of the loan offered to you may be reduced.

The surveyor may suggest to the lender that they withhold some money that will only be paid out when renovation work has been carried out satisfactorily.

If substantial amounts are involved it could be worth getting a second opinion, or renegotiating the price with the seller. Always try and use a surveyor used to dealing with the type of house you are buying. If he gives a low valuation, you will be able to go back to the seller and ask them to knock some more off the price to cover the cost of work he recommends.

Get quotes from local builders – word-of-mouth recommendations are best.

A valuation for mortgage purposes will not tell you whether the house you are buying is structurally sound.

Expect to pay up to £200.

Homebuyer's Survey

This should comment on the condition of parts of the property that are easily accessible. But you won't get a full investigation on possible defects.

It should, however, mention problems that are likely to need work and when. It also mentions problems which do not seriously reduce the property's value, but which might still deter a buyer.

It provides the buyer with an accurate snapshot of the property, warts and all, and ensures he is buying with peace of mind. It is suitable for most properties built after the turn of the century.

Expect to pay up to £250.

Full Structural Survey

In addition to the lender's survey you may want to have a more thorough full structural survey carried out on the property, especially if it's an old house in an area prone to subsidence. It will generally be cheapest if you ask the lender's valuer to do this for you at the same time as acting for the lender.

Alternatively call the Royal Institute of Chartered Surveyors for a member firm local to you.

Another option is to ask friends or your solicitor or estate agent to recommend one.

There's a chance you'll have to fork out for a few of these during your house-hunting. On the back of one, you may decide the house is unsuitable. But equally you may be gazumped or the seller may take the property off the market, which means you'll have to start house-hunting all over again.

Make sure when you appoint someone that you draw their attention to areas of the house you want them to pay particular attention to. They should delve into the cellar and the loft, check on dampness in the walls and climb on to the roof, if possible.

Once you have appointed a surveyor you should receive written confirmation of the work he intends carrying out.

Some people believe structural surveys are only necessary on old properties. But new ones could have major defects too.

Expect to pay over £500.

What the Survey Should Include

As well as a general description of the property and the materials used, there should be comments on the condition of the roof (all gutters, slates, tiles, chimney stacks, etc.), the walls (pointing, insulation, any cracks, dampness, bulges, etc.), the foundations (damp-proof courses, subsidence or settlement, etc.), windows (the state of the frames), floors (the soundness of timber, any dry rot, woodworm, ventilation, etc.), the plumbing (waste pipes, tanks and cylinders), the drains, the electrical wiring and the garden and outbuildings.

Once you have the report, don't hesitate to call the surveyor to discuss it and don't be frightened to ask about any technical terms you don't understand.

You will be able to use the report as a negotiating tool with the seller.

So if any defects have been noted, ask the surveyor how much he thinks they will cost to put right.

Then try and get the seller to knock this off the price of the house.

Guarantees

If the seller hands you a bunch of guarantees for work carried out, maybe for damp-proofing or wood rot, don't take them at face value.

Check that the firm that carried out the work and gave the guarantee is still in business.

If it isn't, the guarantee isn't worth the paper it's written on, although some may be backed by insurance.

If they have gone bust you will be well within your rights to ask for a reduction in the price.

If the guarantee is still in force, contact the firm and find out if it can be transferred from one owner to the next.

You should be able to, but you may have to pay a small registration fee.

Home Improvement Grants

Very few people realise it but local authorities do have the ability to hand out grants to help towards improving homes.

To qualify you generally must have lived in the property you want to buy for at least three years, but not in all cases.

They are also means-tested, so your income will be taken into account in deciding whether you qualify or how much you get.

If you are disabled and will need to adapt the property for your needs and are registered disabled, you could apply for a disabled facilities grant.

A Home Repair Assistance grant is available to people in receipt of income-related benefits and to the over-60s, disabled or infirm. The grant can be used for repair, improvement or adaptation but is generally limited to £2000 or £4000 over three years.

The Department of the Environment, Transport and the Regions has three free leaflets which should be available from your local authority: *House Renovation Grants, Disabled Facilities Grant* and *Home Repair Assistance.*

If you do apply don't go ahead with any work until you get permission from the local authority.

Planning Permission

If you want to make major alterations to the house you don't have to wait until you have bought it before applying for planning permission. In fact, it makes sense to apply early as it can sometimes take weeks or even months to come through.

However, if the house sale doesn't go through you will have lost money in applying.

Forms are available at your local planning office. Normally permission is only required if you are carrying out work that will change the look of the outside of the property. But it's worth enquiring about other work you plan, just in case.

The Department of the Environment, Transport and the Regions publishes a useful free booklet, *Planning Permission: A Guide for Householders*, which should be available at your local council office or Citizens' Advice Bureaux and Housing Advice Centres.

There is also a booklet, *Planning Appeals*, which tells you what you can do if your application has been refused.

Another source of information is the Royal Town Planning Institute's leaflet, *Where to find Planning Advice*, which should help you find a local architect or consultant.

Getting Professional Advice

If you want considerable repairs done or alterations and modifications, it's worth getting to know local architects, building surveyors or property consultants in the area.

They will offer a range of services from preliminary discussions, preparation of designs, applications for approval from local authorities. You can either make use of their full range of services or just choose to seek professional advice at different stages.

Check the fees first. Will they be charged as a percentage of the total cost – which can't be known until the work is finished – or on an hourly basis? They should give you a good indication of the likely cost. Get it put in writing to avoid any misunderstanding.

With any professional you must make sure they have adequate insurance and are members of a professional body which has a code of conduct and complaints procedure if things go wrong.

The Institute of Civil Engineers now has a contract for home extension work to eliminate possible misunderstanding.

If you just want to employ a builder, the best way of finding a good one is by word-of-mouth recommendation. The local estate agent or your neighbours should be able to put you in touch with one.

Some builders put their names on boards outside the homes they are working in. If you like the look of what they are doing ask for a quote and for references. If they are any good they should be more than happy to show you work they have carried out elsewhere.

The Federation of Master Builders could be contacted for member firms. Those on the National Register of Warranted Builders are bound by a code of practice and offer a warranty that defects arising within two years due to faulty workmanship or materials will be put right by that builder or another registered builder.

The warranty also provides up to £10,000 towards any reasonable additional costs if the builder goes bust while your work is in progress.

Members of the Building Employers' Confederation also participate in a guarantee scheme which includes a six-month defects liability and a further two-year guarantee period covering structural defects and some cover if the builder goes bankrupt.

Make sure you get at least three quotes from builders. Write a list of the work you want carried out, so that each one can quote for exactly the same job.

If you are simply looking for a reliable tradesperson there are a number of schemes that will put you in touch with an 'approved tradesperson'. They offer either a free referral service or one where you pay an annual fee that covers a limited number of emergency call-outs and some labour and parts.

All the companies claim that firms on their books are thoroughly vetted, are visited at least annually and that they operate a complaints procedure.

The Automobile Association runs three schemes for household emergencies. Home Assistance Action Desk is a free service for AA members and provides the name of a tradesperson who will work at set rates. It also runs two Home Assistance schemes which offer free emergency call-out and some free labour. Prices start at £59 a year for AA members.

Green Flag Home Assist also has two levels of emergency cover, starting at £96 a year. It guarantees assistance within 90 minutes and includes three hours of labour and up to £100 of materials.

Barclaycard Home Assist is a free service for Barclaycard holders. In an emergency customers are charged £50 for the call-out and the first hour's labour and then given a quote for the rest of the work. It also provides a referral service for non-emergencies.

7

SIGNED, SEALED, DELIVERED

Once you are happy with surveys, the mortgage is in place, and you and the solicitor are happy with the searches, etc., you should get down to serious hard bargaining.

Hard Bargaining

On the back of the surveys you may want to go back to the seller and negotiate a cheaper price or at least ask for a few extras to be thrown in. Curtains and carpets are a good starting point. You may not actually like them much. But having them means you can move in comfortably while you arrange your own colour schemes and make or have your own curtains made.

Whatever happens it is vital to establish clearly items which are and aren't included. In principle, anything that is part of the fabric of the house is included.

Fixtures are generally items which if removed would cause damage, such as electrical sockets, wall switches and wiring, or garden sheds that aren't freestanding.

Fittings include dishwashers, fridges, heaters connected only by plugs, and garden furniture.

Uncertain items include curtain rails and tracks, shelves, and wall lights.

AGREEING TERMS: Tick items included or excluded in the sale

WINDOWS	Included	Excluded
Double glazing	☐	☐
Curtains	☐	☐
Curtain rails and rings	☐	☐
Curtain tracks and fittings	☐	☐
Pelmets	☐	☐
Blinds	☐	☐

ELECTRICAL	Included	Excluded
Immersion heater	☐	☐
Switches, points	☐	☐
Wall and ceiling fittings	☐	☐
Night storage heaters	☐	☐
Fitted electrical fire	☐	☐
TV aerial	☐	☐

BATHROOM	Included	Excluded
Bathroom cabinet	☐	☐
Bathroom heater	☐	☐
Towel rail	☐	☐
Toilet roll holder	☐	☐
Heated towel rail	☐	☐
Mirror	☐	☐

KITCHEN	Included	Excluded
Kitchen cupboards	☐	☐
Wall utensils	☐	☐

GARDEN	Included	Excluded
Greenhouse	☐	☐
Garden shed	☐	☐
Garden trees, shrubs, plants	☐	☐
Flowers and garden produce	☐	☐
Garden ornaments	☐	☐
Garden furniture	☐	☐

GENERAL	Included	Excluded
Fitted carpets	☐	☐
Fitted mirrors	☐	☐
Door bell	☐	☐
Door chimes	☐	☐
Heating oil	☐	☐
Solid fuel	☐	☐
Fitted gas fire	☐	☐
Fitted shelves	☐	☐

ANY OTHERS (list below)

_____
_____
_____
_____
_____
_____

With the seller you should draw up a room-by-room list of exactly what is going and what is staying. The solicitor should use the Law Society's detailed Transaction Protocol and the seller should be asked to complete a detailed fixtures, fittings and contents form which forms part of the contract and is legally binding on the seller. You may also want to make an offer on items the seller didn't plan to leave behind but that you may want.

The Transaction Protocol is a scheme drawn up by the Law Society. It is the seller's solicitor who decides whether it will be used. If so, he must provide:

- a draft contract
- copies of earlier title deeds (if unregistered) or official copies of the entries in the register (if registered)
- a special form of preliminary enquiries called the property information form
- the local authority search and any other appropriate searches (the cost of the searches is paid for initially by the seller, but if the transaction goes through the cost is reimbursed by the buyer on completion)
- a fixtures, fittings and contents form listing all the fixtures and fittings which are included in the price and those which will be removed by the seller

Items Generally Not Removable

- plumbing and heating installations which are not connected by plug
- gas or electric water heaters
- electric sockets, wall switches and wiring
- garden sheds and greenhouses built on foundations
- trees and shrubs

Items Generally Removable

- free-standing gas or electric cooker

- fridge, freezer
- dishwasher, washing machine or other detachable appliance
- heaters connected to mains supply by plug
- electrical fittings beyond the point of contact with mains supply
- lampshades and light bulbs
- carpets and underlay and felt, curtains
- free-standing garden furniture and sheds

Uncertain Items

- curtain rails and tracks, pelmets
- fitted bookshelves and other shelving
- built-in kitchen units/appliances
- built-in cupboards and wardrobes/bedroom furniture
- electric storage heaters, water softener, wall lights
- decorative door furniture and door chimes
- bathroom fittings, lavatory paper holders
- roof TV aerial/satellite dish
- plants in the garden
- free-standing garden ornaments

Offer Accepted

Once your offer has been accepted, the house is 'under offer' and the seller should be asked to agree not to see any other buyers. Check that the house isn't on the market with another estate agent, or you could find yourself pipped at the post by someone else.

During the period between making an offer and exchanging contracts, neither the buyer nor seller has entered into a legally binding contract. As long as the buyer's offer is still subject to contract, the agent handling the sale is under a duty to pass on to the seller all other offers right up to the day contracts are exchanged.

So there is no room for complacency.

If you are outbid, don't give up all hope. It is not uncommon for the successful bidder to have to withdraw from the transaction, perhaps because the sale of their own property has fallen through. So keep in touch with the sellers and let them know how keen you are on the property.

Notify your mortgage lender immediately. You will need to complete the application form and find out when a mortgage valuation on the house can be done.

You may also want to instruct its surveyor to carry out a full structural survey at the same time. If not, you need to appoint a surveyor. Give him details of any part of the property you want him to pay particular attention to and negotiate a fee. Confirm your offer in writing to the estate agent and give your solicitor a copy of the letter. Return your mortgage application letter with the fee for the valuation.

Step-by-Step

● Contact the mortgage lender, complete the application for a mortgage, ask when the valuation can be done and the name of the surveyor if you want him or her to do a report for you at the same time.

● Confirm your offer in writing 'subject to contract and to survey' to the seller direct or to the estate agent. Copy it to your own solicitor or conveyancer.

● Return the mortgage application form with the fee for the valuation.

● Let your solicitor or conveyancer have relevant details of any potential problems. Find out when the seller can move out.

● If your own survey is required, contact the surveyor, discuss the extent of the survey, draw attention to any aspects of the building you are uneasy about. And agree a fee for the work.

The Chain

Even as a first-time buyer or where you have already sold a property there is every likelihood of falling victim to a chain.

The seller may be buying from someone who has a house to sell, and if their deal falls through it's likely to affect yours.

When a problem occurs in the chain, it affects all those in it. And the longer the chain the greater chance of the deal collapsing.

There is not an enormous amount you can do about it. But it does help if a seller is selling through an agent who operates a chain-breaking scheme. Here the agent arranges to buy the seller's house at a discounted price based on a valuation arranged by the agent, so that the rest of the chain can continue.

The house is later sold by the agent, who recoups his or her expenses from the proceeds of the sale. If the house is eventually sold for more than the agreed valuation, the difference usually goes to the original seller.

Gazumping

This is the practice where a seller, tempted by a higher offer, goes back on the deal you thought you had struck and accepts the better offer. It is common when house prices are rising and there are more buyers than sellers.

Despite the fact that buying your home is probably the most important contract you will make, you get very little legal protection. At the time of writing gazumping was perfectly legal. But the government is considering outlawing the practice.

One possible way round it is to get the seller to agree not to sell to anyone else, provided contracts are exchanged within a specified period. This is known as a 'lockout' agreement. The downside is that you could be locked into buying before you've had time to check the property out.

In Scotland the law protects buyers more. There, once a sealed bid has been accepted, the deal is binding.

The Law Society Commission has recommended a pre-contract deposit agreement, designed to help deal with gazumping problems.

The idea is that both the seller and the buyer pay a preliminary deposit of 0.5 per cent of the purchase price to a stakeholder (a third party such as an estate agent or solicitor) and signs an agreement that there will be a final exchange of contracts within four weeks.

If one side withdraws, both deposits are released to the other. So a gazumped buyer would at least have some compensation for the costs incurred.

Another option which has been put into practice by some solicitors is that the seller gives the buyer the exclusive right to buy the house in return for a fee and on condition that contracts are exchanged within a specified time.

One last tip. If you can exchange contracts very soon after your offer has been accepted, your chances of being gazumped are reduced.

It helps therefore to be organised. Before you make an offer make sure you have a solicitor lined up ready to help with conveyancing. And get your mortgage arranged in advance. Once your offer has been accepted get a survey done straight away.

Then just keep pushing everyone until the deal goes through.

Gazundering

This happens in a falling market. Here a buyer drops the price he is prepared to pay just before contracts are about to be exchanged in the hope that the seller will accept it rather than lose the sale of the house.

Exchange of Contracts

The run-up to exchanging contracts is a nail-biting time. So it's essential you:

● Stay in contact with your solicitor to go through the paperwork and sign the contract.

● Check that your finances are in place and your loan offer has been received.

● Make sure your solicitor knows about everything you want included in the contract. Never rely on a gentleman's agreement, get everything in writing.

● Pay the deposit to your solicitor.

● Talk to the seller about a possible completion date.

● If you both have a date in mind, make provisional arrangements with a removal firm.

● The date for completion must be agreed at the time contracts are exchanged. So don't go ahead unless you are sure you can meet it.

The complex financial arrangements involved in house transfer mean you will probably move and complete on the same day. So it's worth preparing a contingency plan just in case things go wrong and you have arranged to move out of where you are staying, but for some reason can't move in as planned.

Exchange of contracts is when documents are physically handed over. If you are buying, a contract with your signature will be sent to the seller's solicitor at the same time the same contract signed by the seller arrives with your solicitor.

It is at this stage that you are legally bound to go through with the deal. You have to buy even if you lose your job or have a change of heart.

So before you sign do ensure:

● Enquiries and searches have been carried out.

● You are happy with any surveyor's report.

● That the mortgage is all sorted.

● That you have a deposit of 10 per cent of the purchase price or whatever you have agreed.

● That all agreements between the buyer and seller are settled.

Don't rely on goodwill. If disputes occur later, the courts will rely on what is written in the contract.

The Deposit

On exchange of contracts a deposit has to be paid by the buyer to the seller. The deposit is non-refundable and is used as security for the contract. So, if you pull out, you lose the cash. The deposit will be deducted from the balance that has to be paid on completion.

Normally it will be sent to the seller's solicitor. If you don't have the ready cash for a deposit, you may have to arrange a bridging loan which will be paid off when you receive the mortgage loan. But this should be avoided where possible. Any delays will mean hefty interest payments.

Completion Day

Today's the day you have to hand over the rest of the money you owe and in return get the keys to your new house.

Your solicitor will normally make the final payment to the seller's solicitor.

When the payments are made, the deeds will be handed over although if you are taking on a mortgage, these will be kept by the mortgage lender, as security for the money being lent.

You won't normally have to put in an appearance at the solicitor's. If the same solicitor is acting for you and the lender it's likely they will deduct from the mortgage advance their own fee and any disbursements (the charges he pays on your behalf like stamp duty and Land Registry fees).

It is normally a condition of the mortgage that on completion the solicitor should have sufficient money to pay the stamp duty and Land Registry fees. So it's important to make sure you have the cash on that day.

You may be charged interest from the date on which the loan

leaves the lender even if it is not used for a few days. However, some lenders will charge only from the date of completion.

Make sure your solicitor doesn't ask for the money too soon.

If you are using savings to pay for part of the purchase make sure your solicitor has a cleared cheque or a banker's draft. This is a cheque signed by a bank manager, or one of his or her staff on behalf of the bank, instead of the customer. It cannot be stopped so in effect is the equivalent to cash.

On completion your solicitor should make the final payment to the seller's solicitor by sending the money by telegraphic transfer from one bank to another. The fee for this is around £20 plus VAT.

When the final payments are made, the deeds will be handed over, although as mentioned before, they will be held by your lender if you have a mortgage as security for the loan.

On the same day you will have to settle up with your solicitor and possibly pay to the lender the first premium on your house insurance, on your endowment policy, the premium for mortgage indemnity insurance (if you needed it and it isn't being added to the loan) and the lender's solicitor's charge if the same solicitor is not acting for you and the lender.

8

THE BIG MOVE

Fixing a Date

Most completions take place on a Friday at the end of the month. This gives you the whole weekend to get settled without too much disruption to your work.

But it's not necessarily ideal. If you make appointments for your cooker to be connected on that day and no-one turns up you could be without hot food for the whole weekend.

Try and avoid bank holiday weekends for the same reason.

Removals tend to be heavily booked at the beginning and end of the month. So you may stand a better chance of getting the firm you want if you opt for a date in the middle of the month.

Countdown to Completion

Insurance

As soon as contracts are exchanged, check with your solicitor that transaction protocol is being used. If it isn't, the house may no longer be at the seller's risk for insurance purposes and you will need to arrange building cover on it yourself.

Even if you don't have to do this, now is the time to start shopping around for buildings and contents insurance (see Chapter 9). If you already have cover where you are living, ask for it to be transferred from the day you move in. And make sure your belongings are covered 'in transit' in case of breakages during removal.

If you are changing insurers, ask for a refund of your premiums if you paid annually for cover. If you paid monthly, organise cancelling your direct debit or altering it if the sum insured is changing but you are sticking with the same insurer.

Other important people to contact are your motor insurer, life insurer and travel insurer – if you have an annual policy (see Chapter 9).

Services

Notify the local authority you are moving into so you can be registered for council tax and put on the electoral roll and billed for water charges.

You will also need to arrange for electricity and gas meters to be read on the day you leave the property you are currently occupying. Give plenty of notice and confirm that they are still coming the day before you move.

Make sure you will be connected and billed from your new address. The seller should organise for bills to be read when they leave, but it's worth double-checking that this will be done.

If you have a washing machine, dishwasher or other electrical appliance, it could be worth booking a plumber or electrician, where necessary, to connect you on the day you move.

If you hire a TV and/or video check whether you can take it with you, or arrange to have it picked up and take out a new contract locally for another one. And make sure you notify the National TV Licence Records Office in Bristol of your change of address.

Likewise the passport office, the DVLC for your driving licence, etc.

Telephone

It is worth talking to the seller to save unnecessary disconnnection and reconnection charges or having to be without a phone for any length of time. Find out whether they are leaving telephones.

Contact the sales office in your new area and let them know whether you plan to take over an existing line, whether you want a new number, etc. If you take over an existing line there is no takeover charge but if it is broken for just one day you will have to pay a fee.

If you are moving within the same telephone exchange area, you may be able to take your existing number with you. But you will be charged for this too.

If there is no telephone line or you need another one putting in there is an installation charge. The number of a new line is often not given out until after installation which could delay your change of address notifications.

Appliances

Make sure the seller leaves details (instruction manuals, guarantees, etc.) of any appliance they are leaving behind. And get them to tell you exactly where the mains switches are.

Accounts

You will also need to contact your bank and notify them of your change of address, That goes too for any savings accounts or National Savings you hold, such as Premium Bonds.

If you want to move your account to a local branch your manager should be able to arrange it for you, but will probably need you to put it in writing.

Mail Redirection

Even if you write personally to everyone who you have ever had dealings with it's highly likely someone will forget your new address.

To ensure your mail reaches you it's money well spent to sign up for the Post Office's redirection service. It charges £6 for one month, £13 for three months and £30 for up to one year. If you want to ensure parcels are passed on, the charge is generally equal to the original postage.

CHANGE OF ADDRESS CHECKLIST - WHO TO NOTIFY

- Bank
- Building society
- National Savings
- Investments
- Share registrars
- DSS
- National Insurance
- Inland Revenue
- Credit, store card and HP firms
- Insurers (motor, travel, house, medical, life)
- AA, RAC or other motoring organisation
- DVLC
- Doctor
- Dentist
- Optician
- Hospital
- Gym
- Employer
- Trade Unions, professional bodies
- TV licence and rental firms
- Phone supplier
- Maintenance contractor
- Schools
- Clubs, societies, book clubs
- Charities
- Mail order firms
- Family
- Friends
- Council tax office
- Publications/subscriptions

You must give seven days' notice before the date you want the redirection to start.

The request form must be signed by all those in the household who want their mail redirected and a separate fee is payable per surname if there is more than one. For details, telephone (0345) 777888.

Keys

However much you trust the seller, it's often a good idea to change the locks on a new house.

Contact a local security firm or buy a new lock to be fitted yourself. Make sure the seller leaves the keys labelled for the doors and cupboards they belong to.

Once you have done this go through your address book and

any files you have for other contact numbers you may have forgotten.

Remember, the bulk of the billions of unclaimed premium bond prizes, unclaimed share dividends, etc., is because firms have lost track of where people live. So make sure you don't fall victim.

Likewise, try and remember firms or organisations you may have contacted only recently and are waiting to hear from.

Make sure you leave a few change of address cards at the place you are leaving and ask the new occupants to send letters on. It won't cost them anything.

Even the postal services redirection service may let a few slip through the net.

Arranging the Move

If you decide to move yourself, look into the costs involved. Where long distances and several journeys are involved it may be worth hiring professionals.

If you do use a removal firm, check the contract so you are clear on exactly what the firm will do and what happens if any of your goods get damaged in transit. Your own home contents policy may cover you for a move. Check and make sure before paying premiums for extra insurance through a removal firm.

If you are moving from a large city to a smaller area, removers from the place you are moving to could be cheaper.

Also think about whether you want the removers to do the packing for you or whether you can do it yourself.

When you ask for an estimate don't accept one over the phone. A good firm will send someone round to gauge the quantity and size of the furniture involved. They will be able to judge how many vanloads and men will be needed for the job. Charges may be based on the time taken to pack and move or may be based on an hourly rate, by half-a-day or a whole day.

You could cut down on the cost by agreeing to do some of the packing yourself and if the move is only a short distance you could also arrange to transport some of your belongings yourself by car.

When you get an estimate make sure you discuss pictures, audio equipment, records, collections of valuables, antiques or fragile items, books, the freezer, plants, etc.

Remember, neither the removal firm nor their insurers will accept responsibility for damage to goods in transit which they have not packed. And, remember, once you have agreed on a quote and a date for the move, if you cancel you are likely to incur a cancellation fee.

If no-one can recommend a particular removal firm use one that is a member of the British Association of Removers (telephone (0181) 861 3331). Get at least three quotes.

If you are keen to move yourself, remember, it will be physically exhausting. You will need strong and willing helpers, plenty of time to do the packing *and* it's only practical for moves over short distances. You'll need lots of boxes, rope, blankets and other protection for polished surfaces.

Things To Do

Hire removal boxes or tea chests for packing if they are not supplied by the removal firm. Alternatively, start paying regular visits to your local supermarket for some.

Start packing things you won't immediately need.

Arrange for the professional disconnection of gas cookers and any other appliances you are taking with you (give seven days' notice).

Arrange for the final reading of gas/electricity/water meters (give 48 hours' notice).

Arrange for your final telephone bill and a telephone disconnection at your new home.

Cancel standing orders or direct debits from your bank account in favour of your existing home (mortgage, gas, electricity payments).

Cancel deliveries of papers, milk and so on and pay off your accounts.

Defrost the fridge/freezer. If moving with a freezer full of food, turn it up before the move.

Clear Out

Moving house is the best opportunity for getting rid of unwanted possessions.

But before you bag everything up and throw it on the nearest tip, think about whether you could sell any of it and whether any would be suitable for a jumble sale or charity shop.

Old pieces of furniture that won't sit well in your new place could be worth advertising in a local paper, for example.

Moving Tips

Draw up a plan showing where you want your furniture. This saves you the trouble of moving it yourself later. Millions of sticky labels will be really useful to attach to each box or piece of furniture.

Throw out clothes and things you don't need. Some removal firms support Oxfam and have an OXBOXX scheme whereby you put all your unwanted goods in boxes, labelling them. The removal company will then deliver them to the nearest Oxfam.

On the day, pack one box with a kettle, tea bags, mugs, coffee, milk and snacks. Matches, kitchen roll, can opener, sharp knife, cutlery, plates, screwdriver, candles, loo rolls and light bulbs are also a good idea. Keep this box with you along with important documents, telephone numbers, cash and valuables and the keys to your new home.

Label boxes and tea chests showing which rooms they should be put in.

On the day of the move, turn off water, gas, electricity, boiler and all appliances and make a note of the readings on the meters.

Arrange with the Post Office to have your mail redirected to your new home.

Action Plan

Four Weeks To Go

- Get removal firm estimates or quotes for van hire.
- Arrange for meters to be read and disconnection at your old place and reconnection at the new.
- Notify telephone sales office of when you want your phone to be read and account closed.
- If renting, confirm written notice with your landlord.
- Start collecting boxes and packing cases.
- Make sure your home contents insurance covers you for the move.
- Arrange extra rubbish disposal if necessary.
- Arrange for post to be redirected.

A Week To Go

- Confirm removal arrangements.
- Start sorting and packing things up.
- Settle paper and milk bills.
- Defrost the fridge.
- Make arrangements for children?
- Book pets into kennels?
- Draw diagram of house for location of furniture.
- Send out change of address cards or order printing after new telephone number is known.
- Confirm account changes at bank.

YOUR MOVE SURVIVAL KIT

Kettle	Dustpan and brush
Mugs	Cloths
Milk	Bin liners
Tea/coffee	Bulbs
Washing-up bowl	Fuses
Detergent	Torch
Soap	Basic tools (screwdriver, hammer)
Rubber gloves	Candles and matches
Mop	Bottle of champagne
Loo paper	

● Arrange for milk and paper deliveries at new address.

24 Hours To Go

● Finish packing everything, bar overnight essentials.
● Confirm timings of disconnection/reconnection at old and new place.
● Keep important documents relevant to the move in a special folder.
● Contact seller about keys, electricity, water, gas, etc.
● Prepare a survival kit.

- Switch freezer to maximum (if moving it with contents in).
- Get a supply of cash (tips, take-aways, petrol, coins for telephone).
- Put dust sheets down in the hall to protect carpets.

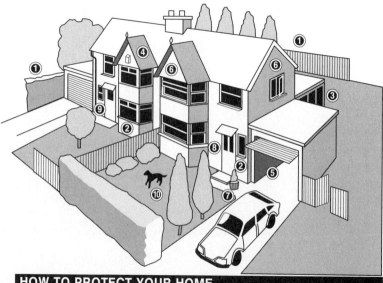

HOW TO PROTECT YOUR HOME

(1) A high wall or fence at the back of a house can put off a burglar, with any side entrances fitted with lockable gates. Trellising and prickly shrubs such as berberis or a thorny rose are additional deterrents.

(2) All ground floor windows and other accessible first floor windows should be fitted with window locks. Most DIY stores stock a selection of these locks. Louvre windows are especially vulnerable because the slats can be removed from the frame. Specialist advice should be sought.

(3) Specialist locks are available for patio doors, seek advice from your installer or specialist and ensure an anti-theft device is fitted.

(4) Visible burglar alarms will deter opportunist thieves. If in doubt about what you need, ask a reputable security firm for advice and quotes.

(5) Lock garden doors and garden sheds. Not only could the thief steal equipment, he could also use it to break into your house.

(6) Never leave a window open when the house is empty. Although you might consider the window inaccessible, a burglar could use a ladder.

(7) Do not hide spare keys outside the house. The first place a thief will look is under pots near the front door, inside the letter box or under the doormat.

(8) Front and back doors of solid core construction should be fitted with a five lever deadlock, which can only be opened with a key. Even if a burglar manages to get in they will not be able to leave through the door without a key. Do not keep spare keys in an obvious spot near your doors.

(9) A light which switches on in response to movement nearby makes it more difficult for the burglar to remain hidden near your house at night.

(10) Dogs are good companions and may give early warning of someone approaching your house.

Source: Age Concern

On the Day

● Pack the van.

● Roll up carpets.

● Check you have left nothing behind.

● Lock the door and leave keys for new owners.

● Collect keys and move into your new home.

How To Protect Your Home

It may be the last thing on your mind, but security is paramount when you move. Eighty per cent of burglaries are carried out by opportunists thieves.

And it's a good idea to have the locks changed. You don't know who the previous owners gave keys to! Make sure you fit locks that are approved by insurers to keep your premiums down.

It could also be worth putting in a call to the crime prevention officer at your local police station.

9

Protecting Against Disaster

Buildings Insurance

From the day you exchange contracts on a property the most important insurance you have to consider is buildings insurance. This is a legal requirement. It covers you against part of the property falling down and having to be rebuilt.

But too many people believe you have to buy it from your mortgage lender. You don't. Unless your mortgage deal ties you to taking out the lender's cover you are free to shop around.

A survey by AA Insurance shows that huge savings can be made by shopping around. Flatowners are the biggest gainers and could save up to 78 per cent while the average house owner could cut the cost of cover by 34 per cent. That means an average saving of over £70.

Most mortgage lenders charge up to £25 if you want to buy a policy elsewhere, but plenty of insurers, such as Direct Line and AA Insurance, are willing to pay that fee for you if you switch to them.

Talk to an insurance broker and call round a number of direct insurers for the best deal.

Premiums for buildings insurance can be as low as £1.50 per £1000 of cover for low risk areas. But that can rise to as much as £5 per £1000 of cover where risks are higher.

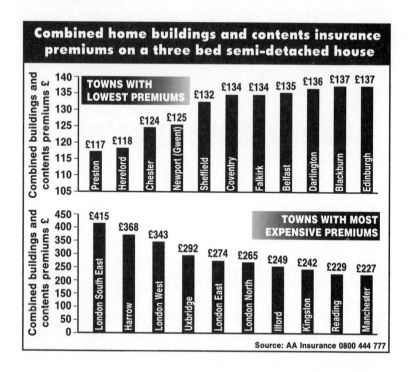

Combined home buildings and contents insurance premiums on a three bed semi-detached house

TOWNS WITH LOWEST PREMIUMS

Town	Premium
Preston	£117
Hereford	£118
Chester	£124
Newport (Gwent)	£125
Sheffield	£132
Coventry	£134
Falkirk	£134
Belfast	£135
Darlington	£136
Blackburn	£137
Edinburgh	£137

TOWNS WITH MOST EXPENSIVE PREMIUMS

Town	Premium
London South East	£415
Harrow	£368
London West	£343
Uxbridge	£292
London East	£274
London North	£265
Ilford	£249
Kingston	£242
Reading	£229
Manchester	£227

Source: AA Insurance 0800 444 777

Subsidence

If the property you buy has been underpinned because of past subsidence problems, you may have problems finding a buildings insurer willing to take on the risk of the problem not resurfacing. In fact, some mortgage companies are wary of offering loans to buy houses affected by subsidence because they know buyers will find it difficult to obtain buildings insurance.

If you live on Britain's clay belt, which basically runs south of a line running from Bristol to the Wash, you could have problems. In fact, in areas considered high risk, an excess – the first part of a claim you have to pay for – for subsidence is likely to be around £1000. That's because the cost of fully underpinning a detached house can cost more than £15,000.

When the last subsidence crisis was at its height in the early 1990s, homeowners who had changed insurer were caught up in disputes over which company was responsible for paying the claim. In response, the Association of British Insurers was forced to lay down rules to make it clear where the liability lay.

The Subsidence Claims Advisory Bureau (SCAB), formed in 1992 to increase awareness of subsidence problems, could help if you are having problems making a claim, getting insurance or have noticed cracks in your new property.

It can find experts to analyse houses and help find insurance for properties that have been underpinned. It has a PUPS (Previously Underpinned Properties) insurance policy backed by CNA Insurance.

Usually at the heart of the problem are trees or shrubs growing close to a property. The Buildings Research Establishment's latest research shows that nearly eight-in-ten subsidence claims on clay soils are a result of trees or shrubs. So make sure you don't fall victim to a tree. See the subsidence illustration overleaf.

SCAB reckons more than two million people are paying over the odds for buildings insurance, just because their homes are on clay soil. It says insurers are wrong to assume that ALL homes are at risk of cracking up because they're in a clay belt.

'It's too much of a broad brushstroke approach,' said SCAB's Chris Jordan. 'Insurance firms fail to take account of what the property is like or where any trees are.

'If you live in one of the 243 high-risk postcodes you could be paying twice as much as someone living in a house not built on clay.'

SCAB now has its own check-up system, which could slash your bill for cover. It costs £15 and gives such information as whether the house is on a slope, its general condition and the position of any trees. SCAB suggests you wave it under your insurer's nose and then demand a premium refund.

'Some insurers have agreed to cut their premiums in so-called bad subsidence areas by up to 40 per cent if our survey shows no major risk,' said Mr Jordan.

You can contact SCAB on (01424) 733727.

Association of Specialist Underpinning Contractors (01252)

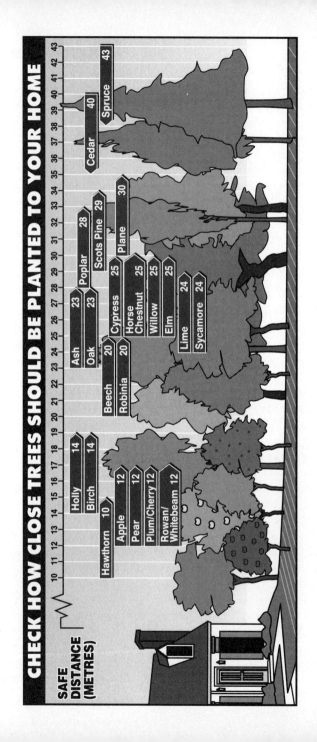

336318; Institute of Structural Engineers (0171) 235 4535; Subsidence Claims Advisory Bureau (01424) 733727.

Subsidence Danger Signs

● Cracks running diagonally on walls or around door and window frames, especially if they are wider at one end than the other.

● Sloping floors and jammed doors also set warning bells ringing.

● The worst-hit homes are those built between 1940 and 1970.

● Homes with cellars and basements tend to be less of a risk.

● Deciduous wide-leaved trees need more water than evergreens, but some conifers can be dangerously thirsty.

● Willows can absorb up to 40,000 gallons of water a year.

Contents Insurance

All it takes is a leaky pipe or a burglar to wipe out the treasured possessions you have spent a lifetime building up.

Yet one-in-four homeowners still risk all by failing to buy home contents cover. It may not replace family heirlooms, but will help you get back on your feet.

The more you pay for cover the more comprehensive the policy should be. You can add accidental damage and cover for belongings away from the home on top of the standard fire, theft and flooding cover.

Cover is based either on the number of bedrooms or you can tot up the total cost of replacing everything in your house. It's important to keep the figure up to date. Wedding presents or the arrival of a baby and all that goes with it can substantially increase the value of your home contents.

You can choose either 'old for new', which will pay out the full

ESTIMATING CONTENTS INSURANCE

	Lounge	Dining room	Kitchen	Landing Hall Stairs	Main bedroom /Loft	2nd Bedroom	3rd Bedroom	4th Bedroom	Bathroom /Toilet	Garage /Shed	TOTALS
Carpets, rugs and floor coverings											
Furniture: tables, chairs, stools, settees, cabinets, sideboards, bookcases. Bedroom, bathroom and kitchen furniture											
Soft furnishings, curtains and their fittings, cushions											
Televisions, videos and audio/visual equipment											
Household appliances: cooker, fridge/freezer, washing machine, vacuum cleaner, electrical goods, heaters											
Cooking utensils, cutlery, china, glass, food, drink											
Valuables: gold and silver articles, jewellery, furs, pictures, clocks, watches, cameras, ornaments, collections											
Sports equipment, books, cycles, records, computers, tapes, toys, musical instruments											
Garden furniture, lawn mowers, ladders, tools, paint, fuel											
Household linen: table linen, towels, bedding											
Clothing											
Other items											

cost of buying a new TV, etc., or you can choose cheaper indemnity cover, which will deduct something for depreciation.

But it's important to shop around and check the policy small print.

What you pay will depend on where you live. The higher the crime rate in your area, the more you're likely to pay. In fact, a recent survey found that a three-bedroom semi in a low-risk area costs £92, while in central London it rises to £147.

If you can't afford this, ask an insurer for economy cover. Some, like direct insurer Churchill, offer cover that costs about a third less. You are covered for the major disasters, but wouldn't be covered against things like falling trees, aerials, contents being moved during removal, food in the freezer going off or stolen keys.

There are plenty of other ways to drive down the costs without cutting the level of cover.

- Join a neighbourhood watch scheme, fit approved locks to windows and doors or a burglar alarm.
- Agree to pay a higher excess (the first part of any claim).
- Look for an insurer that pays a no-claims discount for claim-free years or a loyalty bonus if you renew with them each year.
- Some insurers charge less for older people who tend to be at home more.
- Others will give you a discount if you buy another insurance policy – say, motor – from them.
- Fit a smoke detector.
- Always shop around when your policy comes up for renewal. And consider switching from cover provided by your mortgage lender which tends to be very expensive.

Car Insurance

When you move house remember to tell your motor insurer. Where you live can have a dramatic effect on your premiums. If it's in an area with a high crime rate you are likely to pay more. But if you have a garage or have off-street parking you could pay less.

Alternatively you must let your insurer know if you no longer have a garage. If your car is stolen or broken into and your policy states that you park it in a garage the insurer may not pay out.

Other things that could affect what you pay are mileage. If this drops dramatically because you now live near work or will no longer use the car for work and instead take the train, tell your insurer your annual expected mileage.

Mortgage Protection Insurance

A mortgage is most people's biggest monthly expense. And the consequences of not being able to pay it are dire. Long-term arrears eventually lead to repossession.

Even Hilary Armstrong, the Housing Minister, has warned homebuyers that they cannot expect the state to foot the bill if they are unable to keep up with mortgage payments due to illness or unemployment.

If you want to insure your payments against redundancy or having an accident or being too ill to work, consider a payment protection policy. Only one-in-five borrowers has one despite the fact that the last government slashed help with mortgage payments.

For mortgages taken out after October 1995, it will only start paying mortgage interest payments (not an endowment) after nine months. So, even if you haven't moved house but have switched your mortgage to another lender you will be hit by the new rules.

Most lenders offer protection policies. But they can be pricey, averaging £5 per £100 of cover or £25 a month for a mortgage costing £500 a month. In fact, on a typical £50,000 loan with Britain's biggest lender, the Halifax, you would spend £2,546.33 over the 25-year life of the loan, assuming an interest rate of 8.5 per cent.

But you don't have to buy from your lender, so shop around.

Cover is becoming more widely available to the self-employed and contract workers.

But check for exclusions. Most policies are riddled with them. So, read the small print before you sign up. Often cover isn't available to contract workers or the self-employed. And there is always a delay before they pay out and then the cover only lasts for about a year.

Think about how much financial support you would get from work if you were sick, or how long a redundancy pay-off could tide you over.

Agreeing a longer delay before payments start will help cut the premiums. Excluding unemployment and opting for just sickness and accident cover will also cut costs.

What you pay will depend on your job and health. That said, premiums vary widely. Try your own lender first. Often cover is thrown in free with mortgage deals, especially for first-time buyers, and you can extend the cover to include such things as household bills, such as council tax.

With time it is likely these types of insurance policy will get cheaper. In the meantime, if you are put off by the cost, other solutions might be more cost effective.

Instead of paying for a policy, you could invest the same amount into a building society to build up a 'rainy day' emergency fund. If you don't lose your job, you've lost nothing.

Buying an easily saleable house is also important. It means if times get tough, you can trade down or get out of the market quickly if necessary.

Life Insurance

Most lenders will want you to take out some form of life cover, be it an endowment or simple term assurance. This means the mortgage will be paid off if you or your partner die during the term of the loan.

Endowments are dealt with in Chapter 3. But better by far in my view is term assurance.

It is life cover in its simplest and cheapest form.

It pays out a tax-free lump sum if you die during a pre-set term. There is no savings element. If you survive the term, you get nothing.

Unlike endowments, which combine life insurance with investment and attract hefty penalties if you switch provider within the term of the policy, with term assurance you can switch provider at any time.

Convertible term assurance is similar to level term cover. But the policyholder has the chance to convert the policy into another life policy – perhaps whole of life cover or an endowment – without the need of another medical.

What you pay for life insurance depends on your age, sex and health.

Its cheapest form is decreasing term assurance, where the level of cover falls in line with your outstanding mortgage debt.

Some life insurers will expect you to have a medical. But not always. And it won't necessarily mean you pay a higher premium.

Consider index-linking the policy. This means you are protecting against inflation, which could seriously eat into the value of any payout. Even at 3 per cent a year, the value of your cover will have fallen by 26 per cent after 10 years in real terms and 45 per cent after 20 years. In other words, £100 today would be worth just £74 after 10 years and £55 after 20.

And always make sure the term assurance policy is written in trust.

This means it won't be included in your estate and be liable to inheritance tax and that it will go automatically to your family.

Typically the cost of providing £50,000 of cover over 25 years for a 20-year-old non-smoking male is just £3.75 a month.

There are numerous companies which will scour the market to find the best policy to suit your needs. They include Term Direct and Chartwell Investment Management (01225) 446 556.

But also call a few of the direct insurers such as Virgin Direct, Direct Line and Marks & Spencer. Their arrival into the market has driven down the costs of premiums in the last few years.

Buying Direct or Through a Broker?

Direct insurers say they can usually offer the cheapest insurance because they don't have overheads, such as a branch network, to support.

Brokers point out that they can scour the market for the best deal.

So, the best idea is to call a few direct insurers *and* a few brokers!

10

HOME IMPROVEMENTS

No-one wants to dampen your joy at moving in to your new home.

But be prepared for the fact that there is likely to be much more work to do on it than you ever anticipated. Unless, of course, you are moving into a brand-new house.

Once the rooms are empty, there may be stains on the walls where pictures have been taken down, scuffs on the paintwork and so on. Likewise, rugs may have hidden marks on the carpets.

You may already have planned numerous jobs on getting the house into the shape you want it. Whether it means getting the builders in or doing a little DIY yourself, plan your work carefully.

And always think ahead before you embark on any major 'improvement'. Stone cladding the walls of a Victorian terrace may increase its appeal to you ... but could knock thousands off its value when you want to sell!

If you spend £2500 on a more efficient central heating system, you're likely to get most of your cash back from reduced bills or the increased sale value of your house. But the same amount spent on landscape gardening will save you nothing – and add little to the sale price.

Whether you live in Hull or Huntingdon, Liverpool or London, it's not wise to improve your property way above the standards of neighbouring houses. Estate agents say location is everything – and that means the street where you live, rather than the region.

So don't expect to get back your money if you spend £30,000

doing up a £30,000 terraced house. Especially if the rest of the street is still selling for £30,000. Always try to keep improvements in keeping with the style of the property and those around it.

Last year we spent £6600 million doing up our homes. Top of the list is double glazing, according to a survey by the Halifax. Next is a new fitted kitchen, followed by garden landscaping, home security and a new bathroom.

These are the things the experts say will more than pay for themselves when you come to sell and increase the saleability of your house.

Value Added

Will Increase the Value a Lot

1. Two-storey extension
2. Central heating
3. Garage
4. New kitchen

Will Increase the Value a Little

5. Conservatory
6. Off-road parking
7. En suite bathroom
8. Loft conversion
9. Double glazing on a modern house
10. New white bathroom suite
11. Landscaped garden
12. Original fireplaces

Will Make No Difference

13. Replace sash windows with PVC-u ones
14. Redecorate in neutral shades
15. Swimming pool
16. Paint exterior woodwork
17. Roof insulation
18. Redecorate in distinctive shades
19. Hanging baskets and window boxes
20. Knock through rooms

Added Saleability

Will Make Selling Much Easier

1. Central heating
2. New kitchen
3. Garage
4. Off-road parking
5. Double glazing on a modern house
6. New white bathroom suite
7. En suite bathroom

Will Make Selling a Little Easier

8. Paint exterior paintwork
9. Landscaped garden
10. Conservatory
11. Two-storey extension
12. Original fireplaces
13. Redecorate in neutral shades
14. Loft conversion

15. Hanging baskets and window boxes

Will Make No Difference

16. Roof insulation
17. Replace sash windows with PVC-u ones
18. Redecorate in distinctive shades
19. Knock through rooms
20. Swimming pool

Central Heating

This is the best investment you can make. It costs around £2500 for a six-radiator gas central heating system for a three-bed semi, but you'll easily recoup that cost when you move.

Garage

This will add security and can cut your car insurance bills as well. It will cost from £5000 but you should get that back on selling, especially if garages are hard to come by in your area. A simple stand-alone garage can cost anything from £2000 to £7000.

New Bathroom

Over a million people in Britain still have an outdoor toilet, and every year around two million people renew their bathrooms. At around £600, it's money well spent and should increase your house's saleability. But painting it dayglow purple may not appeal to a buyer! So, keep it simple.

Fitted Kitchen

Giving your kitchen a fresh new look needn't cost more than £2500 to £4000. If you spend more, don't expect to recoup the price. Your dream kitchen may be a monstrosity to a buyer. Make sure the base units are good quality, the finish simple and that it's easy to keep clean.

Double Glazing

Another good investment and still the most popular home improvement.

Always make sure at least one upstairs window opens sufficiently to allow an escape in case of fire.

It can cost from £3000 to more than £10,000 if you're doing the whole house. But it will help cut your fuel bills.

Try to get replicas of existing windows. Changing the look of the house can dramatically reduce its value. And avoid cheap DIY glazing installed by cowboys. It could create condensation, which could cost the same again to put right.

Extensions

Have become a popular option for people finding it hard to move. But make sure any addition is in keeping with your home's appearance. And bear in mind that your home's value is also dictated by the neighbourhood.

Expect to pay around £50 a square foot for the new room. Not only will it improve your quality of life but you can console yourself that it would have cost you £5000 in fees and other expenses to change house.

Loft Conversion

This is fine if you need extra space but it will add little to your home's value. The typical cost is £7000 but you're unlikely to get back more than a third of that when you sell, unless space is a premium in the area you live. But it can also dramatically improve your quality of life.

Insulation

Fitting roof and cavity wall insulation will add little value to your home, but it will save you cash on heating bills (see page 115).

Security

Eight out of ten homes lack adequate protection. So fitting extra security is not a bad idea. Burglar alarms, window locks and mortice locks are generally the best buys. Most insurers offer discounts of up to 15 per cent on home insurance premiums for well protected homes. But always make sure the locks and alarms you fit are on their list of approved devices before you splash out.

Swimming Pool

Building a pool can actually detract from a home's value. Not everyone wants the hassle and maintenance costs involved and they can be dangerous for small children.

Conservatory

You can spend up to £10,000 on a conservatory. But unless it's in keeping with the look of the house, don't do it. If it creates more living space (say you add radiators and electric lights), you could recover half of your costs. Take advice from a designer – you may need planning permission.

Decorating

A lick of paint could be all your house needs to attract that elusive buyer. Doing up the whole house costs from around £100 DIY to £1500+ for a professional job. But be sympathetic with original features. And don't pay a fortune for wallpaper. Only exterior painting costs are likely to be recouped.

Garden

For around £3000 you can add improvements such as a patio, fish pond, shrubs and good fencing. It makes your house attractive, but it's debatable whether it adds value.

STICK TO THE HOUSE RULES

- Take advice from an architect or surveyor for larger jobs.
- Find out if you need planning permission or building regulations approval and whether you can get a grant.
- Get estimates and quotes in writing from at least two firms.
- Get a written contract which includes full details of prices, cancellation rights and guarantees of when the work will start and finish.
- Be careful about parting with money in advance. Query price increases and ask why they were not included in the estimate.
- Act quickly if a problem crops up. Get advice from your local Trading Standards Department, Citizen's Advice Bureau or Consumer Advice Centre.

Save Energy ... Save Pounds

When you move in, you will want to keep costs to a minimum. And there are scores of measures you can take to keep bills to a minimum.

The government-funded Energy Saving Trust reckons if you live in a three-bed semi, you could potentially save £278 a year by fitting energy-efficient products.

And most don't have to cost a bomb.

Hippos are blue plastic bags, often available free from your water authority. You put them round the ballcock in the toilet cistern to cut the amount of water used per flush from nine to six litres.

Turning your thermostat down by just one degree centigrade will save you about £50 a year, while turning your TV off rather than leaving it on standby will save around £10 a year.

Half of a household's energy bills go towards central heating.

By installing a condensing boiler – which is 30 per cent more efficient than boilers over 15 years old – you could slash up to £120 a year off your bill. Although they are more expensive than standard boilers, you should recoup the cost of your investment within three years.

MAKE YOUR HOME ENERGY EFFICIENT

APPLIANCES
Look for the Energy Label to find the most efficient machine
WASHING MACHINES
TUMBLE DRIERS
FRIDGES
FREEZERS

GLAZING
DOUBLE GLAZING
Savings (£15 - 35 per year)

LIGHTING
ENERGY SAVING LIGHTBULBS
Savings (£10 per year, £50 for life of bulb - typically 8 years)

HEATING
HEATING CONTROLS
Savings (£25 - 120 per year)*
HIGH EFFICIENCY BOILERS
Savings (£100 - 130 per year)

INSULATION
LOFT INSULATION
Savings (£60 - 70 per year)
CAVITY WALL INSULATION
Savings (£60 - 70 per year)
EXTERNAL WALL INSULATION
Savings (£85 - 120 per year)
DRAFT PROOFING
Savings (£10 - 20 per year)
FLOOR INSULATION
Savings (£5 - 15 per year)

**Figures based on a three-bed semi

At the time of writing, the government-funded Energy Saving Trust was giving up to £200 cashback if you buy from one of its participating installers. And to maximise savings, if you upgrade your heating controls at the same time, you can get up to £180 off the cost, cut your heating bills by 20 per cent, saving up to £90 a year.

Over a third of the heat we use escapes through the walls.

If you have cavity walls (as generally homes built after 1920 do) you can cut your fuel bills by a third by installing cavity wall insulation. You'll pay around £400 for a terraced house and up to £650 on a detached house. But within five years it should have paid for itself.

A quarter of your home's warmth escapes through the roof. Insulating the loft of a three-bed semi will cost between £200 and £280, but will save up to £45 a year off your annual fuel bill for years to come.

Before you contemplate any energy efficiency measure, check whether you qualify for grants or discounts.

Low income families and the over-60s should contact the Home Energy Efficiency Scheme on (0800) 0720150.

Save . . . Save . . . Save

- Put six inches of insulation in your loft and cut your heating bill by £45 a year.
- Install double glazing, and save £30 a year.
- Put aluminium foil behind the radiators to reflect heat back into the room.
- Use cooler temperatures in your washing machine.
- Defrost the fridge/freezer regularly.
- Use manual instead of power tools in the garden.
- Don't leave your TV on standby.
- Use fluorescent or other low energy bulbs.

Last year trading standards departments reported more than 1500 complaints each week relating to home improvements. To avoid many of the pitfalls follow these six easy steps:

Rules and Regulations

Many projects will need to satisfy Building Regulations which ensure the work is structurally sound. If the appearance of your house is likely to be changed you may also need planning permission. Check with your local authority before you start. Contact the planning department for planning permission enquiries and the building control department for building regulations.

Finding Someone To Do the Job

A word-of-mouth recommendation is the best way to find a good builder, carpenter or plumber. If your friends can't help, look for similar work being carried out in the area and ask the owner if they're happy with the work being carried out.

Alternatively make sure you ask a builder for references and check them out. If you use an architect or building surveyor to oversee the work, make sure they specialise in the type of work you want them to oversee.

Trade Associations

These will be able to give you names and addresses of tradespeople in your area. Some also offer help with complaints and run arbitration schemes.

Package Deals

For some bigger jobs, like fitting a kitchen, a conservatory or a loft conversion, companies will offer a package deal for taking care of everything. It may be convenient but won't necessarily be cheap.

Getting a Quote

You should always try and get at least three quotes for the work. Ask for the quote to include insurance while the work is carried out and any insurance-backed guarantees, how long the quote will remain valid and whether or not it includes VAT (at 17.5 per cent it will make a big difference to the cost). The contractor's terms and conditions should also be made available.

The Contract

This should include a short description of the work being carried out, the agreed price, who will be responsible for getting official approval or planning permission, start and finish dates and any payment agreements. Never, never pay up front for large projects. Pay in stages and consider holding some of the money back for an agreed period after work has finished.

The National Consumer Council's *Controlling the Cowboys* costs £14 from NCC Publications, 20 Grosvenor Gardens, London SW1W 0DH.

The Office of Fair Trading's *Home Improvements Guide* is available free. Telephone (0181) 958 5058.

Borrowing for Home Improvements

Once you've decided to go ahead, finding the money is the next step.

And the answer could be locked away in the bricks and mortar around you. Of Britain's 15.5 million homeowners only 9.8 million have a mortgage, and of those the average outstanding loan is only £27,000.

With the average house price now standing at about £70,000, thousands of people's homes are worth MORE than their mortgages – they have equity in their properties, which they could release to pay for improvements.

A further mortgage advance is the cheapest way to borrow, as interest is charged at the mortgage rate, currently around 8.7 per cent.

Extending your mortgage will involve having your house revalued and you may have to produce estimates of the work you are going to carry out. The maximum you will be able to borrow is 95 per cent of your property's value.

And, remember, it is a secured loan, like a mortgage, so if you fail to make repayments you run the risk of losing your home.

Another option is to remortgage. Here you actually redeem one mortgage and take out another. Remortgaging is more costly, but it doesn't have to be with the same lender. There will be survey and solicitor's fees, mortgage indemnity premiums if you borrow more than 75 per cent of your property's value and possibly even penalty fees for switching your loan.

But if you can take advantage of a more attractive mortgage deal, you will soon recoup the costs and actually save money.

For those with no equity in their property, the next best option is an unsecured personal loan. The interest here is much higher. But personal loans can prove a good option if your home isn't worth much more than your mortgage.

Many lenders offer existing customers preferential rates. So check with them first, before you shop around. To find the best deal, work out the total amount you would have repaid at the end of the loan.

Avoid taking out credit deals from builders or double glazing firms. They often work out much dearer than other loans.

11

SELLING UP

On average we move every seven years. During that time there's every chance you've let the home get into disrepair.

If you want to sell, now's the time to spruce it up. In a sluggish market you will want your property to stand out from the rest. And it doesn't take much cash to make that happen.

It's also important to start gathering information about the property that a buyer is likely to want to see.

First, sort out essential repairs like a leaky roof or downpipe.

You may be able to do these jobs yourself. But if you can't, do allow plenty of time before you want to put the property on the market to get someone in to do the jobs for you.

To start, make a thorough inspection of your house. Look at the place as if you were buying it. What would you notice? The curtains falling off the rails, the damp patch on the ceiling, the missing tile on the bathroom wall!

Draw up a list of jobs that you can do and those that you need professional help with. And set about doing them and ticking them off your list.

Check all the floors. Do they creak, do they need to be cleaned, are there any loose handrails on the stairs?

Check the walls and ceilings. Is the paint and wallpaper in good shape? Are there any holes or cracks that need filling? If the kids have posters on the walls, have the marks ruined the wall-paper?

Check doors and windows. Do they shut properly? Are any door knobs missing or not fixed on properly?

Inspect the bathroom. Are any tiles missing? Does the floor

need a good clean, or limescale removing from the sink and bath?

Similarly, in the kitchen, check for missing or cracked tiles. Is the tap leaking or the cupboard doors falling off their hinges, lightbulbs or switches not working?

Check your attic and cellar. And if they're cluttered, be ruthless in clearing them out.

Then, check outside. The front garden will be especially important. First impressions are everything. Are the gutters in good shape, are the bushes overgrown and the window boxes full of dead flowers? Is the path covered in moss and the outside light switch broken?

After you have drawn up your list, break it down into essential repairs that you can do and those that you need to hire help for. Then compile a list of cleaning jobs you can do and those you need to hire help for.

Essential Repairs

When you think of repairs, don't get carried away. You are unlikely to recoup the money if you decide you need to put in a whole new bathroom. Remember, you won't enjoy any of the benefits but have the hassle while the work is being done.

It's a mistake to think that you can make even more money by fixing up the house. It's likely there is a top price people will pay for a house like yours in your area.

If you have eccentric tastes it could be worth toning them down to sell. Neutral colours sell better than bright ones.

Cleaning Up

If your house is downright dirty and you haven't the time to get it ship-shape yourself, it could be worth hiring a team of dust-busters to come and do the job for you.

Alternatively systematically get down to the job by going through each room with a fine tooth-comb.

The kitchen will be the worst. You'll need to scrub out the oven, the fridge and all the cupboards.

Don't think it won't be worthwhile. It will. Think of the trouble it will save when you come to move.

Tidying Up

Start with the outside. First impressions really matter.

Buyers are going to drive past your house time and time again before they finally commit themselves to the deal. It's unlikely they will pay just one visit. So this is an on-going job.

So, trim the hedges, mow the lawn, make sure the borders are tidy and there is no moss on the path.

Once you've given the back similar treatment, move inside.

Be ruthless. If you have bags of clothes you know in your heart you'll never wear or get into again, send them to a charity shop. Also recycle old magazines and newspapers. Don't simply throw things into drawers. It will pay off in the long term if you sort them out now.

Remember, buyers will want to see in drawers, cupboards, cellars and lofts. And it will help if you already have the house organised before you move. It could be worth investing in stacker boxes – which are cheap cardboard packing boxes – and labelling each one.

There may also be furniture that doesn't fit well in your house, that you never intend taking with you when you move. Getting rid of it now would create a sense of spaciousness that will appeal to a buyer.

Once you've got rid of the clutter think about boxing knick-knacks that mean a lot to you. They may make the house look lived in, but might not appeal to a buyer.

Gather Information

Sit down with 12 months' worth of bills, from electricity and gas to council tax and maintenance bills. Work out what each utility has cost over the year, so that you can tell a buyer how much your home costs to heat and light.

If you have lagged the pipes, insulated the roof, damp-proofed the walls, installed a new boiler, put in a new bathroom, etc., gather the receipts and guarantees of the work done. These could prove a good selling point and it's likely most buyers will want to know about them.

Any warranties for things like ovens that you might leave behind, will also need to be passed on.

Employing an Estate Agent

Scour the area locally and see which agents are used most often. This is probably a reflection on their success rate and the level of service they provide.

Ask for word-of-mouth recommendations too. Once you have identified a number ask them all to come and value your home.

Once you have had a number of quotes, start haggling. Call the agent who suggests the highest price that you are considering choosing a rival firm, because of their high commission rates. There's every chance they will reduce them for you. It's worked for me every time!

Find out what level of service the agent can offer you, what their success rate is and whether they could organise an open day (whereby they gather up potential buyers and show the house to them on the same day). This will probably only be possible if your house is likely to be highly sought after. But it will save the hassle of having to keep it tidy, day in, day out and avoid agents pitching up at your door when you're in the middle of a kiddies' tea party or at bathtime.

What an Estate Agent Should Do

Estate agents don't have the best reputation in the world. But, love them or hate them, they perform an important role. They will have the experience of how properties similar to yours are selling and the likely price it will fetch. They should also be able to suggest any repairs or renovations worth doing before you sell that might help pump up the price.

A good agent should also be able to screen potential buyers well to weed out the nosy and the curious from the serious shoppers. They should also be able to assess whether or not a buyer can actually afford your home.

They will also handle negotiations for you. There is lots of back-and-forth when a deal is being struck, as you will probably remember from when you were buying.

They will act as a mediator. The buyer won't have any qualms telling the agent what they think of your house, but they would probably walk away from it if they had to deal with you. The agent should be able to use his negotiating skills to point out the true value of the house, pointing out other recent sales in your area and so on, something you wouldn't be qualified to do.

The Estate Agent's Fee

You must be told in advance what the estate agent will charge you and also be told if the agent or any of their associates has a personal interest in the property.

Most fees are based on the percentage of the selling price and the type of contract you have with them.

This could be sole agency, where you only give them the business of selling your house. For this you might pay between 1.5 to 2 per cent of the final selling price. So if you sell for £75,000 you can expect to hand over from £1125 to £1500.

By choosing a sole agent you are likely to receive a better service. Joint agency agreements allow you to put your house on the market with a number of agents. But your bill will rise. Expect to pay between 2 and 3.5 per cent or £1500 to £2625 on a house that sells for £75,000.

Charges can vary markedly from area to area and it's well worth trying to negotiate the agent down, especially if houses in your area seem to sell very easily. In some parts of the country fees may be all-inclusive or an agent may charge a reduced fee for selling but add on expenses for advertising and printing your particulars.

Remember, even where an estate agent approaches you saying they have an interested buyer, you will still have to pay his fee.

Also worth remembering is that you'll have to pay VAT (17.5 per cent) on top of the fees.

Selling it Yourself

Everyone does a spot of DIY before selling their home. Carry out the actual sale yourself and it could save you a small fortune.

While it's true estate agents take a lot of the hassle out of advertising and viewing, you do pay for the privilege. Agents typically charge around 2 per cent of the sale price on completion. On a £60,000 property that would cost £1200 excluding VAT at 17.5 per cent. That's why lots of people prefer to save that opting for private sales.

Even if you hire an estate agent on a sole agency basis, you can still sell yourself as long as you haven't handed over 'sole selling rights'. In general, if the agent sells the home for you, you pay up. If you sell it yourself, you don't.

A number of books, guides and kits have come on the market, as more people delve into DIY house transactions, which most good bookshops should stock.

Free ad-sheets, like *Loot* in London, also offer a DIY private sale package for under £60. The deal includes 12 weeks' advertising, an answering service for inquiries, an advice line and a For Sale sign.

Another firm, U-Sell Direct, offers a similar service for under £50. It places ads in free magazines outside London in the South-east, the West Midlands and the North-east.

Estate agents argue it's a false economy. But it doesn't have to be. If you have time on your side and like the sales game, it's worth trying.

But you need to investigate the state of the market in your area well before you set a price. You will need to assess whether a buyer is serious and can afford your house. You must be comfortable with face-to-face negotiating and be able to stand back and even take criticism of your beautiful home.

Selling Tips at a Glance

Do

1. Tidy the front garden, mend the front gate, add colour to empty flower pots. First impressions are everything.
2. Touch up faded or peeling paintwork. Remove rubbish, and put the kids' toys away.
3. Let the sunshine in. Or at least open the windows to get rid of cat, dog and smoking smells.
4. Make the beds, clean the sink, basin, loo, bath and windows and consider cleaning the carpets.
5. Spend a few pounds on fresh flowers and brew some coffee to give the house a warm and homely feel.
6. Keep pets and kids out of the way when you are showing people round.
7. Air the house. But make sure it's warm in winter and cool in summer.
8. Let your viewers enter a room first – it will look less crowded!
9. Make sure you have copies of any main bills for home improvements and guarantees to impress prospective buyers.
10. Switch off the TV. Some soothing background music might not go amiss.

Don't

1. Be too pushy or over-friendly.
2. Give the impression you are desperate to sell . . . even if you are.
3. Mention the neighbours are noisy, unless asked.

4. Offer to throw in any extras like carpets and curtains until you've received a firm offer.

5. Redecorate extensively. The smell of fresh paint may suggest you're trying to cover something up.

6. Let an agent show the house. You should be there too to point out its best features and answer questions.

7. Simply throw your clutter into the loft, cellar and cupboards. Buyers will want to look in them.

8. Lie about any defects in the house. If it has suffered from subsidence, you must say so.

9. Sell it yourself. A good estate agent should be able to keep timewasting Nosy Neds and Curious Caroles at bay.

10. Talk about money. That's the agent's job.

12

CASHING IN ON YOUR HOME

If money is tight, there are numerous ways you can turn your home into a source of extra cash.

Letting

The first is by renting out a spare room. Under the Government's Rent-a-Room scheme which was launched in 1992, you are allowed to earn rent before deduction of any expenses of up to £4250 a year tax-free or £81.73 a week.

If you are jointly letting a room with your husband, wife or partner you can earn £2125.

If you are married or share your home, the income is treated as belonging to the person who actually rents out the room.

The room has to be furnished and in your main home.

If the income you receive exceeds £81.73 a week, you can either pay tax on the extra, with no relief for allowable expenses, or pay tax on the lot and claim expenses for wear and tear and other bills.

If you don't want to sell, you could let the whole house. At the time of writing a study by Black Horse Agencies showed that it can give you a gross return of over 10 per cent of the property's value.

But you must get permission from your mortgage lender and insurer first.

The key to successful letting is to make sure that the property is tastefully decorated, in first-class condition and in a good location.

Remember your insurance company is likely to charge higher premiums than if you live in the property. And there may be times between tenants when the place is empty but you will have to go on paying the mortgage and the bills.

If you have difficulty finding suitable tenants, you could pay an agent to look after the property on your behalf. But this can be expensive.

Go for an agent that belongs to one of the professional bodies – Royal Institution of Chartered Surveyors, The Incorporated Society of Valuers and Auctioneers, the Association of Residential Letting Agents or the National Association of Estate Agents. They should be able to help if things go wrong.

If you want advice on renting, contact the Residential Investment Bureaux. They are located at Quality Street letting agents, a subsidiary of Nationwide Building Society. There are branches in Glasgow, London, Manchester, Bristol and Aberdeen.

Bed & Breakfast

Another option is to offer Bed & Breakfast. Anyone can set up a B&B if they have a spare room. And there is no official registration scheme and there are few regulations if you offer fewer than six beds.

Properties of this size are also exempt from business rates.

Owners must be hygiene conscious because local council inspectors could check that kitchens meet strict standards for food preparation and handling. And if you have more than six beds you will have to meet stringent fire safety regulations.

The downside is that you need to be constantly on hand. You have to make the beds, clean, get up before the guests to make breakfast and be there to say goodbye when they leave.

But you can expect to earn between £20 and £25 a night.

The British Hospitality Association publishes a free booklet on setting up a B&B. Call (0171) 404 7744.

'On Location'

Another less well-known option is to sign up with a film location company and make your home available for a film or TV advertisement. It doesn't have to be a palace. Council flats are in as much demand as mansions.

The Location Company, based in London, is just one of a number of firms specialising in organising locations for TV and photo advertising shoots. But it also does some TV and feature films.

What you will need to provide is plenty of space to accommodate the crew and be situated within the M25 area.

Fees range from £250 and £500 a day for photography and £750 to £1000 a day for filming.

Home Income Plans

More than half of all pensioners depend on state pensions and benefits for at least three-quarters of their income, according to the charity Age Concern.

If you are over 70 and own your home outright, but are in need of extra cash, you don't need to struggle. You can cash in on your home's value with a Home Income Plan. One in two pensioners own their home outright and for many that can provide a vital source of extra income.

A home income plan allows you to borrow money against your home but carry on living there. You have to be at least 69 or a couple must have a combined age of 145 to make it worthwhile.

You take out a mortgage on your home at a fixed interest rate, and the money raised is used to buy a pension called an annuity –

or income for life. The income pays the interest on the loan and the balance goes to you.

Because you still own your home you benefit from any increase in its value. When one or both of you die the loan is repaid from the sale of the house.

Only part of the annuity is taxable. You should also qualify for tax relief at 23 per cent on interest payments on the first £30,000 of the loan at the basic rate of tax. You may even get the relief if you are not a taxpayer. To qualify, your total income, including the interest element of the annuity, must be less than your personal tax allowances.

But you must be wary of who you buy a HIP from.

Risky investment bond-based home income plans were effectively banned in 1990. The plans allowed you to raise cash by mortgaging the home and investing the cash in investment bonds.

The returns from the bonds were supposed to meet the mortgage costs and provide extra income too. But bond values fell, mortgage rates soared and people were saddled with debts on properties that were falling in value.

If you are offered one, avoid it like the plague.

Today's alternatives have in-built security to avoid this problem.

The older you are, the bigger the annuity income you will get.

Because on average a woman's life expectancy is nearly five years more than that of a man of the same age, annuity income is lower for a woman. A man of 70 can expect to live for about 13 or 14 years while a woman of the same age can expect to go on for another 18 or 19 years.

If the same amount of capital is available, the payments to a woman will therefore be spread over a longer period and each one will be smaller. Annuity rates for couples are also lower for the same sort of reasons.

Also, most firms offering HIPs require a minimum property value of £22,000 and for some the minimum is £25,000. The property must be free of any tenants and the building must be in a reasonable state of repair.

As with all investments it's important to take independent legal and financial advice. Important questions to ask include:

● How will my state benefits be affected?

● What if I want to move house in the future?

● What costs will I incur – surveyor's fees, legal costs?

Always make sure the firm is a member of SHIP (Safe Home Income Plans). Its members include Allchurches Life (01452) 526265, Carlyle Life (01222) 371725, Home & Capital (01234) 340511, and Stalwart Assurance (01306) 876581.

They operate a Code of Practice whereby participating firms undertake to provide a fair, safe and complete presentation of their plans to potential clients. An important feature is a certificate which has to be signed by the client's solicitor in every case before a plan can be completed.

Specialist HIP adviser, Hinton & Wild, 374/378 Ewell Road, Surbiton, Surrey KT6 7BB, or telephone (0181) 679 8000, has published a free advice leaflet on home income plans.

Similarly, Age Concern has published a book, *Using Your Home As Capital: a guide to raising cash from the value of your home*, price £4.95. The handbook offers advice and examines the safeguards that exist to protect older people. It is available from good bookshops or Age Concern (0181) 679 8000.

Home Income Plans

Advantages

● As long as you choose a scheme with a fixed rate of mortgage interest, the income derived will remain the same throughout your lifetime. The only factor that could change is a change in the tax rate.

● You remain the owner of your home, which means you benefit from future increases in its value. If it does rise, you have the option of increasing the loan and getting extra income.

● The loan repayable on death will reduce your estate for

inheritance tax purposes and this could decrease or even wipe out any tax that might be payable.

Disadvantages

● The income derived is not index-linked and so won't keep pace with rising prices.

● The income could affect your eligibility for state benefits.

● If you die within a short time of taking out a plan, your estate will suffer.

● You will not normally qualify until you are 69 or, as a couple have joint ages of 145.

Home Reversion Schemes

An alternative to Home Income Plans are Home Reversion Schemes, under which you sell all or part of your home in return for a cash lump sum and the right to continue living there rent free until you die.

Advantages

● These offer a one-off lump sum giving you a substantial sum to invest or spend as you wish.

● With higher value properties the benefits can be much more than with an HIP. The maximum loan with an HIP tends to be £25,000. There tends to be no maximum with a reversion scheme.

● The minimum age is often lower than for a HIP.

● The income is indexed to property values. So if your property value goes up, so does your income.

Disadvantages

● You don't gain from any increase in the property value unless you sell only part of your property.

● Taking out a plan will reduce the value of your estate and therefore the amount you leave to your heirs.

●   The extra income may affect your eligibility for state benefits.

Shared Appreciation Mortgage (SAM)

In 1996 the Bank of Scotland launched the Shared Appreciation Mortgage (SAM).

It allows people to borrow a proportion of the value of their home in return for sharing most of the appreciation in the property with the bank on death. There are two versions. One charges 0 per cent interest. With the other it is 5.75 per cent.

With the 0 per cent deal, the most you can borrow is 25 per cent of the house, whilst the amount of appreciation you will share is 3 times the loan to value (LTV). So if you borrow 20 per cent LTV, you will share 60 per cent of the growth in the value of the house.

This means if a person borrowed £20,000 on a home worth £100,000, which subsequently doubled in value, the bank would get £60,000 from their estate on death.

With the interest-paying version of SAM, the amount of appreciation you share is equal to the loan, which can be up to 75 per cent of the value of the home.

So a house valued at £100,000 would let the owner borrow up to £75,000 on which he or she would pay a fixed interest of 5.75 per cent for the life of the loan.

When the borrower dies, the Bank of Scotland would get 75 per cent of the growth in value. If the house doubled in value, the bank would get £75,000.

With both schemes if the property value falls, the bank gets nothing. One of the advantages for older people is that, unlike some home income plans, the borrower can opt out of the scheme at any time.

Facts About SAM

●   Only properties without existing mortgages are accepted.

●   The minimum valuation is £60,000, the maximum £500,000.

- The minimum loan is £15,000, the maximum £375,000.
- There is a £500 arrangement fee, which can be added to the loan.
- There is an early repayment fee if the mortgage is redeemed within the first three years. This is 1.5 per cent on the interest-free loan or three months' gross interest on the interest-paying version.

JARGON BUSTER

A is for . . .

AA   Automobile Association

ABE   The Association of Building Engineers

ABI   The Association of British Insurers

Advance   The mortgage loan (capital or principal)

APR   Annual Percentage Rate. Laid down by the Consumer Credit Act, 1974, this is supposed to reflect the true cost of borrowing. You'll find it alongside any mortgage rate quoted and it takes into account most of the up-front and on-going costs involved in taking out a mortgage. You can't always rely on it because lenders work it out in different ways

ASI   The Architects and Surveyors Institute

Assignment   The transfer of some kinds of property, like an insurance policy on an endowment mortgage

B is for . . .

B&B   Bed and Breakfast

Balance outstanding   The amount of loan owed at any time.

BAR   The British Association of Removers

BEC   The Building Employers Confederation

Bridging loan   A loan used to cover payment for the purchase of one house, until you receive the proceeds from the sale of your own house

BSA   The Building Societies Association

C is for . . .

C&G   Cheltenham and Gloucester Building Society

Capital   The mortgage loan (advance, principal)

Capital reducing mortgage   Repayment mortgage

Capped rate   An interest rate charged for a set period of months or years which can go up and down with the variable rate, but there is a maximum (capped) rate it can't go above

Cashback   A payment you receive when you take out a mortgage. It may be a fixed amount, or a percentage of the mortgage

Charge Used to denote a debt or a claim for payment

CML Council of Mortgage Lenders

Completion date The finalisation of a contract, the day money is paid and keys handed over

Conditions of sale The standard terms governing the rights and duties of both buyer and seller as laid down in the contract they sign

Contract Agreement to sell a property, not binding until exchange of contracts

Conveyance A written document transferring unregistered property from the seller to buyer

Conveyancing The legal process involved in buying and selling property

Covenant A promise in a deed to undertake or to abstain from doing specified things

CRA Credit Reference Agency

Creditor The lender

D is for ...
Deeds Often called 'title deeds', the documents conferring and providing evidence of ownership. In registered land transactions these will be the Land Certificate or the Charge Certificate

Discounted rate A guaranteed reduction in the standard variable mortgage rate, often over an agreed term

DIY Do-It-Yourself

DVLC Driver and Vehicle Licensing Centre

E is for ...
Early redemption Paying off a loan before the end of the term

Early redemption charge A penalty fee charged to cover administration costs when someone redeems a loan early

Endowment mortgage A loan on which only interest is paid. It is paid off by the proceeds of an endowment policy at the end of the loan term

Exchange of contracts The process of making an agreement to buy and sell a house legally binding

F is for ...
Fimbra Financial Intermediaries, Managers and Brokers Regulatory Association

Fixed rate The interest charged on the mortgage is for a set amount for an agreed period of months or years

FMB The Federation of Master Builders

Freehold This is when you own a property and the land it is on

G is for ...
GAAP Generally Accepted Accounting Practice

H is for ...
HIP   Home Income Plan

HMC   Household Mortgage Corporation

HVCA   The Heating and Ventilating Contractors Association

I is for ...
Index map search   A search to find out if ownership of a property is registered at the Land Registry

Interest only   Your monthly payments to your lender are simply made up of interest. You do not pay any of the mortgage off during the life of the loan. This is done by using the proceeds of a savings policy, an endowment, for example

ISVA   The Incorporated Society of Valuers and Auctioneers

J is for ...
Joint tenants   Two or more people holding property as co-owners

L is for ...
LTV   Loan to Value. This is the size of the mortgage as a percentage of the value of the property or the price you are paying for the property. A £45,000 mortgage on a house worth £50,000 would mean a LTV of 90%

Land certificate   Similar to a log book from the Land Registry, to say you own a house

Land Registry   Government department responsible for keeping a register of all properties in England and Wales which have registered titles

Leasehold   This is when you own a property for a fixed number of years after which it goes back to the freeholder. Most flats in England are leasehold. And although most lenders will lend on leasehold properties, they will demand that there is a number of years left on the lease (typically 60)

Legal charge   In terms of buying a house, the mortgage

Lessee   A person who takes on a lease

Lessor   The landlord who grants a lease

Level term assurance   Life assurance which pays out a lump sum amount if you die during the term. The amount of cover stays the same throughout the term, which makes it suitable for interest-only loans because the debt remains the same over the life of the loan

Local search   Application made to the local authority for a certificate providing information about a property and the surrounding area

Low-cost endowment   A

mortgage secured by a mixture of
an endowment with-profits policy
and decreasing term assurance, so
that the guaranteed sum insured
payable on death is equal to the
loan. The bonuses added to the
endowment each year normally
ensure, but don't guarantee, that
the loan is paid off at the end of
the term

Low start mortgage   Premiums
start low and increase by a certain
percentage each year until the
full level premium is reached

M is for ...
M&S   Marks & Spencer

MIG   Mortgage Indemnity
Guarantee

**MIRAS (Mortgage Interest Relief
At Source)**   This is tax relief on
your mortgage interest payments.
At the moment it is 15 per cent
on the first £30,000 of the loan

Mortgage   A loan for which a
house is used as security or
collateral. It gives lenders certain
rights in the property, including
the right to sell the house if
payments aren't made

Mortgagee   The lender

Mortgagor   The borrower

**Mortgage indemnity
policy**   Insurance required by a
lender for a loan which is above
the percentage of the valuation of
the property at which the society
will normally lend (typically 75 to

80%). Also known as a higher
lending fee

**Mortgage protection
policy**   Insurance taken out to
cover loan repayments in the
event of sickness, unemployment
or disability

N is for ...
NACOSS   National Approval
Council for Security Systems

NAEA   The National Association
of Estate Agents

NAPHMSC   The National
Association of Plumbing, Heating
and Mechanical Services
Contractors

Negative equity   This is where
the money you owe on the
mortgage is greater than the value
of the property. For example, if
you had a £60,000 mortgage on a
property valued at £50,000 you
would have £10,000 negative
equity

NHBC   The National House
Building Council

P is for ...
PAYE   Pay As You Earn

PEP   Personal Equity
Plan.   This is a tax-free way to
own shares or unit trusts.
Depending on the lender, you
can use PEPs to repay an interest-
only loan

Personal pension   This is a
structured personal savings and

investment plan to provide for your financial needs after you retire. You can use some or all of the proceeds from a personal pension to pay off an interest-only mortgage

PIA   Personal Investment Authority

Preliminary enquiries   Questions about a property made before exchange of contracts

Premium   One-off or periodical payment for an insurance policy

Principal   The amount of money that has been borrowed and on which interest is calculated

PUPS   Previously Underpinned Properties (insurance policy)

Purchaser   The buyer

R is for ...
RAC   Royal Automobile Club

Redemption   Paying off a loan in full or in part

Registered land   Land the title to which is registered at the Land Registry

Repayment mortgage   Loan on which part of the capital and part of the interest is paid back throughout the loan term

RIBA   Royal Institute of British Architects

RICS   The Royal Institute of Chartered Surveyors

RSUA   The Royal Society of Ulster Architects

S is for ...
SAM   Shared Appreciation Mortgage

SCAB   Subsidence Claims Advisory Bureau

Sealing fee   A charge made by lenders when you repay the mortgage

SHIP   Safe Home Income Plan

SIB   Securities and Investments Board

Stakeholder   Someone who holds a deposit as a middleman between the buyer and seller

Stamp duty   A tax you pay on properties which cost over £60,000. This is charged at 1 per cent of the purchase price. So, a property costing £67,500 would have stamp duty of £675

Structural survey   The most wide-ranging check of the outside and inside of a property. This is carried out by a professional and should indentify any hidden faults

Subject to contract   The words you should put in every letter to a seller and his or her solicitor or agents before contracts are exchanged

Sum insured   The amount that will be paid out when a term insurance policy matures or the event insured for occurs

Surrender value   The amount of money a policyholder receives if a life insurance policy is terminated before the expiry date

T is for . . .

Tenants in common   Two or more people who together buy a property that does not automatically pass to the surviving tenants in common

Term insurance   A life insurance contract that pays out only on death within a specified period

Term of mortgage   The number of years at the end of which a loan is repaid

Title   The right of ownership of property

Title deeds   Documents referring to ownership of land

Top-up mortgage   Additional mortgage from another lender when the first lender does not provide enough finance to buy a house

Transfer   The Land Registry document transferring the ownership of the property from the seller to the buyer

U is for . . .

Under offer   The term used when an offer on a property has been accepted

V is for . . .

Valuation   A simple check of the property in order to find out how much it is worth and whether it is suitable to lend a mortgage on

VAT   Value Added Tax

Vendor   The seller

WXYZ is for . . .

With-profits policy   A life insurance policy where bonuses are added regularly to the original sum assured and paid when the policy matures

USEFUL CONTACTS

**Architects and Surveyors Institute
(ASI)**
St Mary House
15 St Mary Street
Chippenham
Wiltshire SN15 3WD
Tel. (01249) 444505

Architectural Association
34–36 Bedford Square
London WC1B 3ES
Tel. (0171) 636 0974

**Association of British Insurers
(ABI)**
51 Gresham Street
London EC2V 7HQ
Tel. (0171) 600 3333

**Association of Building Engineers
(ABE)**
Jubilee House
Billing Brook Road
Weston Favell
Northamptonshire NN3 8NW
Tel. (01604) 404121

**Association of Relocation
Agents**
PO Box 108
Edinburgh EH7 5JQ
Tel. (0131) 558 3060

**British Association of Removers
(BAR)**
3 Churchill Court
58 Station Road
North Harrow
Middlesex HA2 7SA
Tel. (0181) 861 3331

**British Insurance and Investment
Brokers Association (BIIBA)**
BIIBA House
14 Bevis Marks
London EC3A 7NT
Tel. (0171) 623 9043

**British Wood Preserving and
Damp-Proofing Association**
6 The Office Village
4 Romford Road
London E15 4EA
Tel. (0181) 519 2588

**Building Employers
Confederation (BEC)**
82 New Cavendish Street
London W1M 8AD
Tel. (0171) 580 5588

**Building Societies Association/
Council of Mortgage Lenders
(BSA/CML)**
3 Savile Row
London W1X 1AF
Tel. (0171) 437 0655

Building Societies Ombudsman
*Investigates most types of complaint,
as listed in a pamphlet*
Grosvenor Gardens House
35–37 Grosvenor Gardens
London SW1X 7AW
Tel. (0171) 931 0044

Controller of Stamps
Stamp Offices
South West Wing
Bush House
Strand
London WC2B 4QN
Tel. (0171) 438 7452
*(counter service only; phone for
address of local offices)*

**Council for Licensed
Conveyancers (CLC)**
16 Glebe Road
Chelmsford
Essex CM1 1QG
Tel. (01245) 349599

**Department of the Environment,
Transport and the Regions**
(Public Enquiry Point)
Eland House
Bressington Place
London SW1E 5PV
Tel. (0171) 890 3000

**Federation of Master Builders
(FMB)**
14/15 Great James Street
London WC1N 3DP
Tel. (0171) 242 7583

**Heating and Ventilating
Contractors Association (HVCA)**
34 Palace Court
London W2 4JG
Tel. (0171) 229 2488

**Incorporated Society of Valuers
and Auctioneers (ISVA)**
3 Cadogan Gate
London SW1X OAS
Tel. (0171) 235 2282

Institute of Plumbing
64 Station Lane
Hornchurch
Essex RM12 6NB
Tel. (01708) 472791

Insurance Ombudsman
*Deals with complaints about most
insurance companies. Set up and
financed by them*
City Gate One
135 Park Street
London SE1 9EA
Tel. (0171) 928 7600

Law Society
113 Chancery Lane
London WC2A 1PL
Tel. (0171) 242 1222

Legal Services Ombudsman
22 Oxford Court
Oxford Street
Manchester M2 3WQ
Tel. (0161) 236 9532

**National Approval Council for
Security Systems (NACOSS)**
Queensgate House
14 Cookham Road
Maidenhead
Berkshire SL6 8AJ
Tel. (01628) 37512

National Association of Estate Agents (NAEA)
Arbon House
21 Jury Street
Warwick
Warwickshire CV34 4FH
Tel. (01926) 496800
or call the Homelink Hotline direct:
(01926) 410785

National Association of Plumbing, Heating and Mechanical Services Contractors (NAPHMSC)
14/15 Ensign House
Ensign Business Centre
Westwood Way
Coventry CV4 8JA
Tel. (01203) 470626

National House Building Council (NHBC)
Buildmark House
Chiltern Avenue
Amersham
Buckinghamshire HP6 5AP
Tel. (01494) 434477

National Solicitors' Network
156 Cromwell Road
London
SW7 4EF
Tel. (0171) 244 6422

Personal Investment Authority (PIA)
The main regulator for personal investment products. Has taken over the regulatory functions of LAUTRO and Fimbra
7th Floor
1 Canada Square
Canary Wharf
London E14 5AZ
Tel. (0171) 538 8860

Royal Institute of British Architects (RIBA)
Client's Advisory Service
66 Portland Place
London WIN 4AD
Tel. (0171) 580 5533

Royal Institute of Chartered Surveyors (RICS)
12 Great George Street
London SW1P 3AD
Tel. (0171) 222 7000

Royal Institution of Chartered Surveyors in Scotland (RICS Scotland)
9 Manor Place
Edinburgh EH3 7DN
Tel. (0131) 225 7078

Royal Society of Architects in Wales
75a Llandennis Road
Rhydypennau
Cardiff CF2 6EE
Tel. (01222) 762215

Royal Society of Ulster Architects (RSUA)
2 Mount Charles
Belfast BT7 1NZ
Tel. (01232) 323760

Securities and Investments Board (SIB)
The SIB is the body which oversees the PIA and other regulatory bodies
Gavrelle House
2–14 Bunhill Row
London EC1Y 8RA
Tel. (0171) 638 1240

SHIP (Safe Home Income Plans) Campaign

SHIP consists of several of the major providers of home income plans and home reversion schemes who have agreed to operate a new Code of Practice. For a free leaflet and further information about SHIP contact:

Cecil Hinton
Secretary
Safe Home Income Plans
Hinton & Wild (Home Plans) Ltd
374–378 Ewell Road
Surbiton
Surrey KT6 7BB
Tel. (0181) 390 8166

INDEX